For Marie —

Here's hoping
you're enjoying
gardening and
garden life.

All the best,
Bill Young
3 Oct. 1998

GARDENING LIFE

LEE MAY

LONGSTREET
Atlanta, Georgia

Published by
LONGSTREET PRESS, INC.
A subsidiary of Cox Newspapers
A subsidiary of Cox Enterprises, Inc.
2140 Newmarket Parkway, Suite 122
Marietta, GA 30067

Printed in the United States of America

1st printing 1998

Library of Congress Catalog Card Number: 98-066364

ISBN: 1-56352-497-X

Jacket illustration and design by Meg Page
Book design by Jill Dible

For Lyn, my Muse and joy

magnolia grandiflora

INTRODUCTION

As far back as I can remember, I have loved and appreciated gardening and life.

With my parents as role models, I have embraced both with gusto — through their many turns, their ups and downs — learning over the years that living and digging in the dirt weave together in a grand and vibrant pattern. All life's lessons grow in the garden: birth, nurturing, love, heartbreak, success, joy and so many more.

In this collection of essays, I look at these lessons through a lens that focuses on the meaning of planting, pruning and watering, yes, but also on how these life-sustaining doings in the garden connect with family, friends, places, music, food, nonconformity, desire, obsession.

More than five decades of living and gardening have taught me much. Nothing more important than the knowledge that ultimately passion, good passion, will triumph. That gardening life as fully as we can fills us with surprise, wonder and hope.

CONTENTS

~

fall
red berry

Nandina domestica

Latin version of Japanese name

PART ONE

SEASONS

Falling leaves, sprouting trees
send signals profound, powerful

~

THE AUTUMN REVIVAL

AFTER MONTHS OF DEFENSIVE gardening, watering furiously just to keep plants alive, I am more than ready for some serious enjoyment. Autumn, my favorite season, is prime time for that.

Unlike its billing as the season of decline, fall is, for me, a time of renewal.

But I wonder if my desire to enjoy the glorious golden days will be overcome by a need to catch up on lost gardening time. It's a battle of urges, similar to the one that takes place after a long, harsh winter, when spring's beauty competes with its suitability as a time for planting.

Throughout the killer summer, with its long run of 90-degree days, autumn's promise helped me slog on. How long can this last? Not long, I asked and answered almost daily as I held the hose, hooked up the sprinkler and hauled buckets of water around my small space.

At times, "Stayin' alive, stayin' alive — ah, ah, ah, ah, stayin' alive" echoed through my head like a theme from some gardening disco flick starring the Bee Gees and John Travolta.

At least it's not an acre, I told myself, ignoring the fact that the smaller the garden, the guiltier you feel if you don't keep everything watered and groomed.

In any case, most of the plants survived, and early this month the ginger lily bloomed, giving the illusion of a crispness that had not yet arrived. That was about the time the Boston ivy began turning red on the brick wall (too bad those bricks aren't gray, I say every year).

Always a garden refresher, fall this year promises to be a reviver, as some plants shut down during the prolonged heat and drought, waiting, hoping, like the rest of us, for a weather break.

Uncharacteristically balky most of the summer, an old clump of hardy begonia in a half barrel finally cranked out pink blossoms, although this indestructible perennial always puts on a fine foliage display with its big angel-wing leaves, green and hairy on top and reddish underneath. Volunteer impatiens growing in a hemlock's pot bloomed this month for the first time — initially one little red flower, then more every few days.

And my oleanders took the middle of September as a signal to produce their first flowers of the season, pink and white.

These late bloomers testify to the restorative powers of autumn — powers that work outside the garden as well as inside it.

My wife, Lyn, is a close, personal example. She wilts in the heat. A few days ago, she began perking up. Along with the nandina.

"When they come to life, that's when I come to life," she says, noting the plants' "beautiful new garments" of reddening leaves and berries.

Most of us darken up our wardrobe this time of year. For her part, Lyn begins wearing colors that bear a striking resemblance to those wine hues in nandina leaves.

To be sure, leaf color is one of the fall garden's stronger attractions, ensuring that you don't have to go to the mountains to enjoy the show. (Here's hoping the drought doesn't dampen the display too much.)

In addition to the ivy, some of our more spectacular players include oakleaf hydrangea and dogwood, their leaves turning burgundy and purple, as the corkscrew willow's become the color of lemon peel.

And just the other day, I noticed that one of my red-twig dogwoods had, seemingly overnight, shed its summer green.

Blooming through the heat and still going strong are the blue balloon flowers, sedum and rose of Sharon. Meanwhile, common hydrangea blooms have gradually turned a wonderful beige, recalling some we saw on the Isle of Wight early one October.

With shorter days, temperatures have no choice but to dip, making it possible to actually stay out in the garden — looking, not just watering.

However, I already can see how tough it's going to be to just enjoy. Gardeners often are like cooks who, after laboring over a dish, have trouble enjoying it without picking through its parts.

I tried just appreciating the other day — taking time to smell the ginger lily — and wound up finding a few spaces that needed filling. So I planted setcreasea, the sprawling purple perennial. Transplanting, put off during the heat, needs doing. A moss garden must be planted.

And, like so many gardeners, I find it virtually impossible to walk through my space without stopping to pull out a weed, errant seedling or sprig of grass.

Afflicted thus, one friend says she gives herself "deadlines," vowing to stop working in the garden at, say, 6:00 P.M., and start enjoying it instead.

Maybe I'll try that. But first, that plot of ajuga needs moving. And the peppermint looks so skanky, it has to be put out of its misery . . .

I can enjoy. I know I can.

September 17, 1993

WINTER UNMASKS ESSENCE

Looking out on my back garden one recent gray day, I could see a cardinal, dressed festively in holiday red, masked for a high-style ball. Perched near the top of a saucer magnolia, it preened away, twisting and turning, like the five parched leaves that incongruously clung to the tree.

Stunningly beautiful, the bird practically glowed in contrast to the somber, misty sky. From time to time it would stop flitting and just sit, staring through the branches, while from inside the house, I stared at it.

This went on for about ten minutes. Then a blue jay swooped toward the tree, lighting on a branch at precisely the time the cardinal flew away. Repeating the cardinal's preening moves, the blue jay flapped its wings happily, stopping occasionally to take in the scenery.

After watching the blue jay for another ten minutes, I went to the front of the house, from where I could see about a dozen more of the usually raucous, much-maligned jays. They were dashing about, soaring and diving, barely missing one another, like trained sky divers, in perfect accord, a bluish blur.

Like the cardinal, the blue jay's color was heightened in the grayness. Just as the garden's essence is more apparent this time of year.

In her book *Edith Henderson's Home Landscape Companion*,

the legendary garden designer calls January "the truthful month. The bone structure of every outdoor area is totally revealed as weak or strong."

If winter is brutally frank, it also is compassionate: neither birds nor plain plants need compete against spring's showy blooms or autumn's spectacular color. Winter is the great leveler.

Undistracted by lushness, I appreciate both the birds and the garden's structure now more than at any other time of year.

In Atlanta, where we can garden virtually every month of the year, winter is the closest thing to downtime that gardeners get. In every other season most of us are tempted and persuaded to get out there and dig and plant and prune and weed.

To be sure, we can do all that during much of winter (I've always loved the answer to the question on when to prune, attributed to a Japanese bonsai master: "Whenever the knife is sharp"). But, if ever there is a time to do nothing to the garden, this is it.

Maybe part of the reason for that is the holiday season, when many workers work not, garden workers included. Or maybe some ancient rhythm winds down and instills in us the knowledge that it is okay to take a break now. Whatever the reason for fiddling less with the garden, I think it's a good thing. I've always thought it unfortunate that gardeners spend so much time making gardens beautiful and so little time enjoying that beauty.

So, each year at this time, I do my part.

I go, easy, to the Japanese maples. Their weeping forms are as striking in their bare beauty as they are with leaves. I look at them and contemplate where and when I might want to make a little snip. The same goes for the other deciduous trees and shrubs, including the ginkgo and dogwoods, the oakleaf hydrangea showing off its peeling, cinnamon-colored stems, the wizened hazelnut, corkscrew willow and crape myrtle, whose bark is so richly colored it resembles vanilla ice cream with chocolate syrup melting through.

Like the cardinal and the lone blue jay, I just look, not even thinking of picking up the pruning shears just yet.

What little blooms now is mercifully discreet — the sweet olive, the twice-blooming Yoshino cherry, a few random yellow flowers on the Carolina jessamine that covers the arbor. Each seems to apologize for interrrupting the season. Their unobtrusiveness fits.

Even the pansy, that iron-strong marathoner whose name has been taken to describe the weak, cooperates. I swear a bed of plants in the front garden has grown to a deeper burgundy since I set them out in November.

With a portion of my garden bare-branched, what is left green — the Japanese black pines, the bamboos, anise, laurel, banana shrub, aucuba, mahonia, ligustrum and others — really stands out. Blobs of green in various shades, floating in a sea of browns and grays.

Winter expands my small garden, as many of the ferns, hostas and other perennials die back and the leafless trees and shrubs take up less space. Here and there a spot opens up, as where the banished but surprisingly resilient houseplant, China doll, dies back each winter, returning in spring.

But no matter how big it gets, my garden gets no work from me this time of year. I will not even rake the leaves. The woods don't get raked, do they?

Now's the time to savor, to anticipate. Soon enough, the ground will be alive with plants I'd forgotten were there, tender tiny things that disappeared long ago. Any day the lenten-rose blossoms will appear for their months-long visit. Before I know it, quince will splash red near the purple hyacinth, the daffodils will blare. Forsythia and spirea, too. The daphne will be blooming and perfuming soon enough.

And that saucer magnolia where the cardinal and the blue jay play will host a million perfect blooms.

January 6, 1995

BABBLE ON, APRIL

Autumn still is my favorite season, but spring is gaining ground.

Maybe it is because aging brings hope and need and desire for renewal — which is most associated with spring. Maybe it is simply that, increasingly, paradoxically, as I age, life feels fresh and new — two attributes associated with spring long before they became cliches among sheeplike fashion mavens.

Whatever the reason, I like this spring more than I have any before.

I've come a long way since the days when I seconded Edna St. Vincent Millay's emotion about spring in her poem named for the season: "It is not enough that yearly, down this hill, April / Comes like an idiot, babbling and strewing flowers."

Babble on, April. Strew me some flowers, baby. And some shrubs and trees, too.

What is strewn this spring will not differ much, ostensibly, from what was scattered across my front and back gardens last year and the year before. But it will feel and be very different because I view the season in such a changed way. The shift must have been building for years, breaking through this year because of a converging of positive events, including my getting deeper and deeper into my fifties, writing my first book and reaching an unprecedented comfort level in relationships with my once-estranged father and my never-estranged wife, Lyn. She who is my last wife.

Now, when Lyn and I take our daily strolls through the garden,

I love seeing the little leaf buds of the Japanese maples opening stickily. This means that, soon after, we will see that perfect burgundy color that even the fashion designers can't duplicate, wish as they may. And, of course, this is the season in which azaleas and rhododendrons bloom and swagger through the garden, riding on confidence that reflects their numbers and popularity around the city. They have a place here.

Like them, I feel at home, too. In the sense that I am attached to our place in Atlanta. And, in the larger sense, attached to the region.

That attachment is strengthened in this season as in no other — the season that crashes through our senses on elephant feet, too impressive to ignore.

Dark loam, looking good and feeling rich, combines with myriad smells of fresh blossoms to make the journey through spring as pleasing to the nose as to the eyes and hands.

On our arbor out back, Carolina jessamine grows up, down, all around, fragrantly yellow, creating a pompadour on top. Its sweeps, dips and curls rival the most creative hairdos. Comparing that fully beautiful scene to the skimpy one several years ago when I first planted two little jessamine plants is a metaphor for the growth of my garden here and to the accompanying growth of my pleasure in it. Both will be six this year.

Maybe that is the explanation for my growing appreciation and fondness for spring: time. Yes, time on earth, time spent gardening life, increases the appreciation of all good things. Or should. And time in one place. Six years in one house. One garden. That is a record, a personal best. Maybe certain feelings need time to jell. Maybe moving around so much, as I did, jangles feelings and diminishes perspective.

Time and perspective came together in the last year as I wrote my autobiography. Sifting through my gardening life, through my relationships, brought everything into sharper focus — including spring's attributes. Now that the book is finished, I have time to enjoy the season. And enjoyment, for me, is a most crucial part of gardening.

I can never be sure that I would have felt the way I do about spring if I had stayed this long in some other place in some other time of my life. While timing is everything, it also works in mysterious ways.

But like some of the past, all that is mercifully moot.

What I do know is how I feel about the season now. Hello, spring.

Hello, April. I love you.

April 7, 1995

WINTER HORROR, SPRING FANTASY

Snuffed in their prime, my saucer magnolia blossoms hang brown and forlorn on the tree, stark testimony to the brutality of winter's last blast, a season that went down as the winter from hell.

The magnolia blossoms are not alone. Nor, of course, am I; brown is the true color of Atlanta's early blooms. Throughout the region, all of us who embraced the warm just before winter's end, declaring it spring, did so knowing we'd get zapped again. Nevertheless, we were shocked and appalled when winter doubled back on us. Again. Knowledge and expectation do not necessarily dull adversity's sting.

"I have never seen a winter this bad, and I'm ninety-eight years old," Dr. Leila Denmark, the beloved pediatrician and envied gardener, said recently as she told me what the windy freeze had done to her Forsyth County rose garden. Like others all around the region, her rosebushes had sensed spring, then gotten smacked by winter, their little red leaves stopped cold.

For every gardener and garden lover, there is a lament.

A friend at the newspaper sent me a computer message filled with passion, reflecting the pain of watching winter stomping on spring's parade. Walking in their usually verdant pre-spring neighborhood, she and her husband encountered a scene that broke her heart: "Burned forsythia, brown Bradford pears, burned crab-apple about-to-be blooms, withered lily leaves, pale daffodil foliage drooping around burned blossoms, camellias that will never open, totally brown gardenia bushes . . . pitiful fruit trees!"

She went on to acknowledge that later bloomers likely will fare well, "but this first burst that is so exhilarating was murdered, and I'm depressed. Have you any Prozac for prevention of dead-spring blues?"

I feel her pain. But I know that she knows that only time will heal us — and many of the plants with murdered blooms, as well.

Only a few days after our exchange of sad messages, we were chatting about the joys of topless cars, knowing that in Georgia, if not the frozen North, warm sunshine was upon us. Resilient, persistent, bloodied but unbowed and unfazed, spring had returned again, making yet another run on winter.

This time, the calendar was on its side.

Yes, that's worth no more than the law on your side when somebody runs a red light and mows you down. But, the fact is, winter always stops. Sooner or later, spring sends it packing, presenting what's left of its own show.

They may be fewer than in some years, but the dogwood and azalea blossoms will light up Atlanta, their treacherous trip enhancing our appreciation. Already, my azaleas have opened a few tentative buds, as have a neighbor's.

My Japanese maples are leafing out, free of post-traumatic

stress. Other trees and shrubs, teased warmly to leaf and bloom, then zapped, are leafing again, matching spring's resilience and toughness.

Lenten rose, whose early blooms were mushed, is putting out new ones, restoring a little bit of spring lost. Browned-leaf gardenia branches still show green when I scratch them, making me as hopeful as a paramedic finding a pulse; maybe I'll get a few of those fragrant, creamy-white blossoms that Billie Holiday loved so sadly.

While the saucer magnolia blooms are gone to brown, the tree is making leaves, moving on, not dwelling on earlier failures.

We people will move on, too. And because we do hope eternally, it doesn't take much to put us in a spring state of mind.

Leila Denmark, or Dr. Leila as she is known to legions of patients and parents from her almost seventy years of baby-doctoring, is there. After last Sunday's deliciously fat weather, she said, "Now, if we can have a few more days like yesterday, things will be fine."

March 29, 1996

MOCKING WINTER'S BLAST

What's going on?

After the long, cold winter, too many early blooms were dying. Now, amid brutal heat, some long-delayed flowers are rising.

Life's going on, somehow reassuring us all.

A couple of weeks ago, I looked out my upstairs back window and saw half a dozen pink and white blossoms on the saucer magnolia — the same tree whose showy blooms were zapped in their prime back in the spring.

The week of the magnolia also was wisteria week.

First I heard from Jane Rosenberg-Coombs of Roswell, who reported a drive-by sighting of wisteria blooms on Holcomb Bridge Road. In July. The next day, Patty Gironda, keeper of the Old Garden Inn in Newnan, told me she was getting her first blooms of the year from an awesome old wisteria whose large trunks snake around a cedar arbor, producing perfumey, purplish blossoms galore.

Of course, none of these late bloomers were as virile as they might have been earlier. But, then, who is?

They were doing what they could; they showed up, putting on what show they had left in them. Not as profuse as in spring, but showier than the traditional scattering of summer flowers. Obviously, they are making up for time and beauty lost. Perhaps it is their iron will that makes us appreciate these July blossoms disproportionately.

Said Jane, "Some things are indomitable. You just can't hold them down. You may get beaten back, but you bloom sometime, even if it's not your designated time."

To be sure, things happen when they're supposed to.

Meanwhile, back at my garden, the wisteria chats resonated. It was just last year that I got my first blooms from a wisteria sapling Frank Stanley and I separated from its rambling parent plant in Marietta. Those purple, majestic blooms were six years coming, not uncommon for wisterias, I'm told.

(I suspect the difficulty in making wisteria bloom in the garden, while it flourishes in the wild, makes some gardeners badmouth it as "trash." That's easier than admitting defeat.)

Thus, when my wisteria broke out in blooms last year, I felt a fine sense of accomplishment — mixed with the realization that, in a garden, you're never in full control; nature can always erase your labors and dreams.

So it was this year when the furious winter came and stayed and overstayed, ignoring the calendar. Apparently, my wisteria was nipped before it budded. I visited the twining vine daily, searching for bud signs, hoping for a repeat of last year's performance.

Nothing happened.

Nothing but the kudzulike growth that wisterias show. By June I could hope no more. I pruned back some new growth to around six leaf buds, preparing for the proverbial next year.

Hope returned when I heard Patty and Jane talk so passionately about the unexpected pleasure of wisteria blooms in July.

If wisteria was blooming north of Atlanta and south of Atlanta, why not in the city? Why not in my back yard?

I went back to my first-blooming wisteria. Still nothing. I began checking the others I'm growing, although they're younger. No buds there, either. One day, I saw a few blooms on a wild wisteria growing along a fence on nearby Ashby Street. My plants remained bare.

Then, the second week of July, on the wisteria twirling along the back-porch rail, I saw it: one bud, swelling toward purple. The blooms it had when I bought it three years ago were all I'd seen. Now this. I checked it often, fearing that too much attention could make a good thing go away.

By last Tuesday, the purple cluster was fully extended, standing tall. And by today, I expect to smell its perfume.

Take that, winter.

July 20, 1996

NATURAL ART OF COLOR

There's nothing like nature to teach garden design. And there's nothing like autumn to show it off.

Some human designers plant with an eye to fall color and structure, but most seem to pick plants and locations with spring in mind — the time when blooms burst out all over, spraying color all around the landscape. Autumn hues (and such rich ones they are — yellows, reds, golds, purples, browns and more) are left mainly to nature to mix and match. What an awe-inspiring job it does.

That came across to me vividly the other day as I spent a long time just looking at the bountiful color of my garden, the color combinations, plants' proximity — all set off by sharp-angled light cutting through crisp air. That I did not plan this autumn joy somehow made it all the better. I couldn't have done it so well on purpose, anyway — just as even the best fashion designers cannot duplicate autumn's naturally beautiful colors.

Through a window on the back porch, ornamental grass — fruiting, yellowing, browning in a black pot — waved in the afternoon breeze, beckoning. I went, then able to see the grass in combination with the very, very red — redder than in spring — leaves of a threadleaf Japanese maple, a companion to two others across the way on the back garden's high side.

The magnolia in a tub looked all the greener amid fall's color, while the rose in a planter next to it still was green, too, with the most sensuous rusty red growing new out of its cane tops.

Standing tall in a big planter along the brick walk, a crape myrtle, whose showy blossoms charm for months, bloomed anew with persimmon-colored leaves that keep on intensifying as the season progresses, color pleasing beyond belief, just as autumn does every year. Next to it, in a smaller pot, my threadleaf (green in spring) maple showed a similar persimmon. Together, what fiery light they cast, while the coleus planted under the maple added a burgundy glow.

Nearby, a rose in a tub still was blooming white, while its new burgundy leaf and stem growth, not seen for months but making a sensational fall appearance, made a perfect match for the chrysanthemum underplantings.

Against the red brick wall, fan-shaped leaves of the little ginkgo hung like golden seashells, promising to shower the ground any day now. The golden ginkgo matched a nearby maple, as well as the surprisingly rich color of the blue balloon flower's persistent leaves. A golden triangle they made.

Dwarf mondo, mostly green, with a few patches of black, lives (reluctantly) in front of my little pond in a hot, sunny space I call Sahara. Autumn brings relief to the shade-loving perennial; now, less beaten by midday sun, the leaves lose their brown stress marks, hailing this merciful sweet autumn.

In the front garden, the yoshino cherry, whose leaves do little for me most of the time, comes alive this season, making up for its normal blandness by turning persimmon, looking good with the golden chrysanthemum planted underneath.

Loropetalum, whose purple leaves already show off much of the year, turns red-orange for autumn, complementing the dogwoods of similar color, while the coral-bark Japanese maple leaves flame out in yellow and blood-orange.

The color purple repeats again and again — in ajuga, shamrock (both revived for fall), barberry, nandina, hydrangea. There's even new purple on the stems of ivy in front-porch hanging baskets.

Walking through the crackling autumn afternoon, through the tapestry growing out of my serendipitous planting and nature's deft design, I took notes for future efforts. But mostly, I took pleasure.

November 15, 1997

SWEET, DANGEROUS ANTICIPATION

This is the time that tries gardeners' souls. The shortest month is the longest wait for gardeners needing to dig in the dirt.

Every year around about now, anticipation rises high and mightily, as many of us see visions of lush greenery dancing in our gardens. In our mind-gardens, the flowers are abloom, the Japanese maple leaves opening red and fuzzy.

Call it pre-spring, this in-between time when early plants gingerly approach the soil's surface while a waning winter lurks, waiting to pounce again.

How sweet the anticipation is. There is something exciting about this time of year, something reassuring, too, as our sleeping passions awake — again — bursting into flower.

The excitement returns each year in myriad ways as we eagerly await the explosion of azalea color, the elegant clouds of dogwood blossoms, the first fern greening through the dark, rich earth. Part of the joy is knowing that all of us — plants and people — have come through another of life's winters, of course. And, for those of us on the high side of fifty, there's the added, and increasingly important, appreciation for another season of renewal.

Amid the excitement, always, there is a touch of danger. Plants that stick their tender faces out of the ground before winter truly is over find that — ZAP! — they've lost their heads. We humans lose our heads in different ways. Unable to resist making our moves too soon, we put in fragile young plants at the rise of a thermometer.

Then, when it falls again, as it inevitably does, so do our hopes of having the lushest, greenest garden ever. Fortunately, hopes, like spring, are resilient; they always rise again. And again.

Ah, anticipation. Where would we be without it? It is a mark of passion. When we no longer look forward to something with so much hope that we can barely stand it, we have lost that certain something. Passion, once so sharp that it cut, has dulled.

How much like life this is: So much sweet anticipation is fraught with danger — or at least the fear of it. Still, we leap, faithfully, into pleasures. At least, we should.

To be sure, no one, not even a gardener, can sustain the fever pitch of passion 365 days a year. We all know what summer will be like. We will drag ourselves to our gardens to water only, unable to dig or prune, unable sometimes to even look with any degree of cool comfort.

But now, with the promise of spring beating wildly in our hearts, the passion of anticipation runs high. I can hardly wait to see whether the creeping fig I've been pampering in an effort to make my wall feel like those in Charleston and Savannah will finally reach the top bricks. Whether the oleander I'm growing will bloom this year, after taking last year off.

What a battle I will see as my rhododendron duel my azalea for showiest plants of the garden. Both will have to go some to beat out the saucer magnolia, whose pinkish-white blooms light up the back like a thousand flashing bulbs. Not to mention the promise of hydrangea — those blue mopheads — which I have increasingly taken a liking to.

All that is to come; the passion will grow hot with spring and summer. Soon.

Now, sweet anticipation reigns. In this in-between time, every garden is always most magical. Lush, verdant. And relationships and love bloom there with the greatest of comfort and joy. Anticipation. Imagination. The mind is a powerful thing.

February 7, 1998

REDISCOVERING SPRING

Spring's touch confirms that life's rhythms have not been silenced, as leaves sprout tender and shoots squirm from the ground in vibrant richness.

To be sure, there were times when I did not cherish spring the way I loved autumn, when I thought it too sweet, too soft. That was when I was twenty-five, with big hair and painful cynicism about my country's civil rights and Vietnam War struggles. Then, I was thirty-five, with a career focus that blinded me to spring. By the time I was forty-five, I could see again — just as I did as a child, when spring championed unbridled youth.

Then, every dandelion was a snowstorm to be blown through the air, every tree a forest beckoning. And we Meridian, Mississippi, boys and girls relished the invitation, the exploration. Best, most seductive, was the mimosa. Its leaves, sensitive, closing at night and in the rain, wove wonderful mysteries around the South. How did they do that? Climbing this tree offered rewards money could never buy. Up in its canopy grew powder-puff blooms that contained the nectar of life. Pluck a bloom, suck this magic potion, as every child in my neighborhood did, and you live forever. Most immediately, you taste the sweetness and tumble to the earth, sated, in merry wonder.

Now that I am fifty-six, I wonder again. And I know. I know the worth of surviving another winter, the beauty of seeing another green season. Another mimosa with mysterious leaves and life-giving blossoms. There's nothing like age to make you value aging.

And the season of renewal. On a recent Sunday, I was driving home to Atlanta from Birmingham on a most perfect spring day — yes, before the calendar made it official. But spring knows no calendar; it comes when it wants to. The blue sky and pinkish cherry blossoms combined to stop my senses in their tracks. Others must have felt it too, as traffic slowed to something approaching reason.

Back home, my saucer magnolia had burst into full flower, its blossoms dotting the sky like pink and white stars. Too, many others light up my garden this time of year — lenten rose, quince, camellia, Carolina jessamine, rosemary, scotch broom, and more. Saucer magnolia, however, is spring's best barometer in the garden. The magnolia reflects spring's vagaries: If the late freeze comes — whoosh! — there go the beautiful blooms, mushed to brown. If spring comes and goes, warm and mellow, the blooms last forever.

Waiting warily to see whether spring acts out is a trap, however. The season is to be enjoyed when it can be. Like life. Fret too much about what spring might do, and you miss its show.

Go outside in the sunshine — or the wet — and you're embraced by the sights, sounds and smells new again. Japanese maple leaves opening red and fuzzy enchant. Standing in a warm, pattering rain the other day, I turned my face up and, transported, felt springs eternal. Paris, as a boy soldier in the 1960s; Meridian, in the '50s, when sweet gums dropped "golf balls" for us impoverished players.

And the blooms, ah, the blooms of spring. One after another, right on through June, they come in waves. On and on. Dogwood and azalea. Rhododendron and hydrangea — two flowers so over the top, so impassioned, so big and much, they epitomize us Southerners: We live large. On to the big, leathery-leafed Southern magnolia, blooming big and sweet.

Sweet, too, is the earth, its fragrance released through slices by trowel and shovel. There's nothing like newly turned earth to excite the gardening senses. And when dark, rich loam, looking and feeling so healthy and vibrant, mingles with the fragrance of banana shrub, native azalea, viburnum, Virginia willow, mock orange, the power overwhelms.

Sweetest of all is spring's air of anticipation. Will my creeping fig, a strong, delicate reminder of Charleston and Savannah walls, really take off this year, reaching the top of my wall? Will wisteria have a good season, blooming purple, full and fragrant? Will life bring great change and surprise?

For so many, spring is a time of relief, pollenated air notwithstanding.

The other day, a friend who is a gardener sounded cheerful on the telephone for the first time in months; she felt better each day, she said, after suffering through what, for her, are winter's dark, depressing days. Seasonal affective disorder, it's called. And for once, an acronym is right on the money. "I'm inspired," said my friend. "Now that it feels like spring, I want to get out there and start planting."

So, what would spring feel like if it didn't have winter to kick around? Following the season of short days and dimmed light, spring is bound to look good, some might argue. But I know spring would be wonderful at any time; it can follow any act. It is its own self.

For me, years of cynicism has been sandwiched between appreciation. Now, again, I know spring's beautiful value. I know it is, ultimately, a season of hope, belief in the possible. Now, the garden of life flourishes with joy and promises to keep. Mimosas to climb.

March 22, 1998

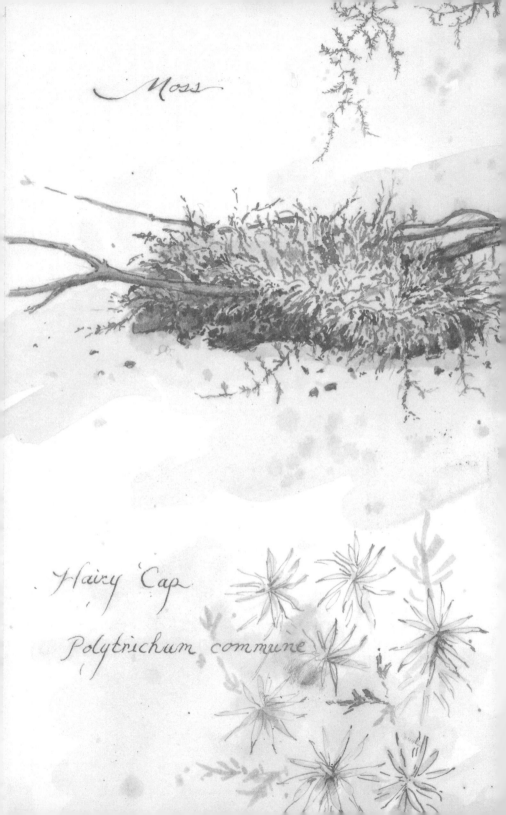

Moss

Hairy Cap

Polytrichum commune

PART TWO

PASSIONS, QUESTS, OBSESSIONS

*A plant, a garden, a desire
will really get a hold on you*

❧

THE MAGIC OF MOSSES

FROM TIME TO TIME, a plant or garden feature really gets a hold on me.

At various times in recent years, I've been under the spell of bamboo, boulders, pines, maples, boxwoods. I couldn't get enough. Each time I found a new specimen, I'd make room for it, even if that meant displacing something else.

Now, mosses are it.

For more than a year, I've been scanning the shoulders of highways, exploring woods and country roads, clambering around stream banks — all in search of another clump of that cool, green stuff.

Often I have taken extreme pleasure at hearing friends curse the moss that "invades" their lawns; that means more for me.

Fern moss from a friend's yard has replaced the liriope that once encircled my saucer magnolia. The liriope had turned into a raggedy skirt, embarrassing the magnolia and crawling onto the surrounding brick. The change makes the space seem cooler, calmer and larger.

Throughout my garden in Atlanta's West End, I have placed moss patches on rocks and under shrubs, enjoying them as they evoke a wonderful sense of deeply serene woods and create little gardens within the garden.

Like ground clouds, mosses look and feel soft, cushy — inviting you to roll around on them. They smell like a mixture of earth, sea and grass.

Mosses are the latest object, but each of my periodic quests is part of gardening's rhythm, providing a sense of change and renewal, helping make my space dynamic. (The trick, of course, is to get enough change and renewal without making the garden look like it was planted yesterday.)

Fortunately, mosses come ready-aged. Their presence suggests stability, constancy — indicating that a space is safe, undisturbed.

And while they are found growing quite well on their own, mosses usually experience a little period of adjustment when I bring them to my back yard. For three weeks or so, I water them daily, often more than once. So far, most of the several varieties I have collected are doing okay, hunkering down to avoid the heat and the blue jays that love to peck and fling.

As my moss space and interest expand, so does my need to know more. For example, what's the best way to make it spread? Should I rip out my Irish moss (not a true moss), which grows in full sun, and replace it with the real thing? What's the best way to grow moss on rocks?

Such questions naturally intrigue botanists who specialize in mosses, prehistoric plants known as bryophytes. Bryologists have counted some ten thousand species of moss. Heightened interest in mosses mirrors general concern about the environment as rain forests disappear and pollution of air and water spreads.

Ann Stoneburner, a botanist at the University of Georgia, says mosses are important ecologically because their leafy surfaces collect seeds from other plants, helping propagate them. Additionally, mosses provide homes for numerous insects and make way for other plants by breaking down rock to create soil.

Dr. Stoneburner and others complain that moss collectors often take too much, depleting this important resource.

"I've spoken to some foresters who use the words 'rape' and 'pillage,'" she says, adding that collectors should always be careful to harvest small sections.

Mosses are undeniably plants of substance, but they are known mostly for their style. And like many styles, they go in and out of fashion.

"Back when people were making terrariums, I saw a lot of moss," says Jay Jones, a garden designer. "Maybe it's like bell-bottoms and hip-huggers — coming back."

Well, yes, there is something retro about mosses. They are simple plants, recalling simpler times. Their uncomplicated nature enhances the role of a garden, any garden, as a pathway to calm and peace.

August 6, 1993

PLANT PARENTHOOD

Emotional ties to plants are binding in so many ways.

I take great pride in the orange tree I grew from a seed tossed into a pot of soil eight years ago one evening after dinner. In some ways it's like a child, a member of the family whose progress I've charted. Similarly, many plants I have received as gifts and through trades provide a wealth of good-time memories.

Then, when a plant dies, the sense of loss can be crushing.

To be sure, I am prone to ripping out plants and replanting others in their spaces. But that's different from losing them to some mysterious ailment, as happened this summer when I discovered that a winter daphne, the evergreen shrub whose sweet fragrance I had enjoyed for three years, was giving up the ghost for no apparent reason.

Like a lover who shows no signs of dissatisfaction, then goes out for a bottle of wine, never to return, daphnes will check out on you without having expressed a shred of discontent.

Speaking of heartbreak, consider the story of Arty Schronce and his orange tree.

It was at the end of September 1992 that Schronce put his miniature orange tree (calamondin) outside to repot it.

"I thought it was well-disguised and nobody would be interested in it," recalls Schronce, who had bought the tree for $1.50 in South Carolina when he was twelve.

Yes, you guessed it. Somebody stole the tree, which for Schronce represented twenty years of emotional investment and attachment.

He put out the word to neighbors to be on the lookout for the missing tree, even putting up notices in his apartment building. Nothing happened.

Then, a month later, as he was driving to work, taking an unaccustomed route, he spied the tree, looking like it had been set out for trash collection — because it had.

How did he recognize the tree?

In the same way you would recognize any loved one you have known for twenty years.

"There it is," Schronce recalls saying to himself. It looked dead.

Schronce, a horticulturist, drove a block, then decided to swing back and pick up the tree so that he could "at least use it as mulch, scatter its remains" in his garden.

But as he retrieved the tree, "Four guys came out of the building, and the ringleader said, 'That's our herb tree.'"

Enraged (perhaps almost as much by the man's calling it an "herb tree" as by having it stolen and discarded), Schronce defied the four men and took back the tree, making a hasty departure, looking over his shoulder all the while.

The episode "did shake me up," Schronce recalls.

Imagine how shook up was Saba Yimam, when she got home several years ago to find all her pothos plants dead. Her apartment, which had been "like a jungle," had become a graveyard.

Her pain and loss were worsened by the fact that she apparently had accidentally killed the plants herself when she drenched them with bug killer.

"I felt bad," she says. "I felt really terrible. I thought I had done something awful."

Yimam worked mightily to save her plants.

"I changed the dirt," she recalls. I bought them some medicine plant food, but the stalks got limp." They were gone.

She says, "They were like babies. It was like losing a member of the family."

Now plastic plants are all she has. "They're not as good," she acknowledges. "One of these days, when I get a home, I will get more live plants."

Back to Arty Schronce.

Instead of making mulch of the little tree, he decided to have a go at reviving it. He watered it and put a plastic bag over it for humidity.

This went on for a while, then near Christmas, he noticed a bud. "It was like a little miracle," says Schronce, who reports that more and more buds appeared and, although it has not borne fruit since its plant-napping, "It's doing fine now."

Schronce is doing fine, too, but still says, "I wonder what adventures the tree must have gone through."

While some people talk to their plants, no one I know has ever reported plants talking back.

However, years ago, when there was a Soviet Union, I recall reading about experiments in which Soviet scientists hooked up machines much like lie detectors and measured plant emotions.

One story said a man who had hacked up a philodendron was paraded in front of the plant victim, causing a huge reaction that was recorded on the machine's graph.

Absent such technology, we can only guess what Schronce's plant suffered and felt.

Whatever they were, at least the orange-tree adventures ended happily.

October 29, 1993

CHASING THE HORSETAIL

"We checked out of our hotel at 9:00 A.M. and had booked a cab to take us to Narkanda, to see a panorama of the Himalayas, then down to Chandigarh via Chail.

"The road was very twisty, and scary in parts. It took about five hours to go a hundred kilometers. The view from Narkanda was spectacular. Most of the road follows high ridges. As the road began to descend from Chail to cross a river, I noticed some springy places and started looking for equisetum. I spotted it, yelled to the driver to get out and ran back to make sure. It was, indeed. My old equisetum eye had not failed me."

That's Richard Hauke, describing in his journal an encounter with a horsetail reed called Equisetum diffusum in the Himalayas twenty years ago. That encounter meant Hauke had, at last, seen all fifteen species of horsetail reed in their natural habitats.

Now that I've talked with Hauke, I'll never again look at a horsetail reed without thinking of India. Or Costa Rica. Or Kenya. These are among the many places Hauke has traveled in search of knowledge about equisetum, often used in plantings in and around ponds.

Hauke (pronounced HOW-ky), a sixty-four-year-old botanist, retired from the University of Rhode Island in 1989 after teaching there for thirty years. Now an Atlanta resident, he has taught at Georgia State University and plans to return to the classroom there in the fall, teaching a course in plant biology.

Throughout his academic career, Hauke, a Detroit native, has stalked the horsetail, which, like ferns, always seems to me prehistoric, conjuring images of long-tailed creatures wading through steaming ooze. But beautiful.

Hauke, who lives in a condominum near downtown with his wife, Kathleen (no, he does not grow equisetum at home), explained that there is a scientific foundation to that prehistoric image. He says that equisetum tells us a lot about how plants have evolved through the ages: "In speculating about the evolution of plants — how did the leaf evolve, how did life cycles evolve — this particular group is still around and tells us something that was going on 350 million years ago."

During a conversation at his home, he went on to talk about the sex lives of equisetum, along with how the plants inform him and other scientists about how seeds got to be the way they are.

That was interesting stuff, I admitted, but I was interested in knowing more about how to grow the reeds (Equisetum hyemale, or winter horsetail), whose green stems with black bands are hollow to the touch. Just the back-yard gardening facts, I all but said.

I've grown horsetail (the name supposedly stems from its roots, which resemble horse hair) for several years, with mixed success. The ones I put in my pond refused to come back in spring. Some I put in the ground apparently got enough sun but not enough water, so they put up stalks only here and there.

Sensing my need to discuss the more mundane aspects of equisetum, Hauke acquiesced, but not before noting that his studies did not center on gardening concerns. "I was doing it as a botanist, not as a horticulturist," he told me.

That said, he did note that in their natural habitats, the reeds often grow where a good underground water supply exists. "They evolved as plants along rivers, where you have constant deposits of sand, then they moved into wet meadows and forests and places like that," he said.

He went on to say, "If you drain between waterings, they don't do very well, because they like to have their feet always wet. I used to grow them in the greenhouse, with the pot in water."

Hauke said that in America, the widest variety of horsetails grows in the North, in places like Michigan, Vermont, New Hampshire and Maine. It seems that the horsetail became more diverse as it moved north from its origin in the southern hemisphere, unlike many plants, which are more diverse near their centers of origin. Of the fifteen species worldwide, eleven are found in North America, north of Mexico, Hauke said, adding that the reeds also are found in South America, East Africa and Southeast Asia.

So, did he grow them as mere laboratory plants, or did he like them personally?

"Oh, I like them," Hauke said, specifically recalling the Equisetum diffusum he gathered in the Himalayas two decades ago. It grew well in pots, he said, adding that he provided some to an Ohio nurseryman who cultivated unusual plants.

"And it turned out that when I got to Atlanta, there was some in the botanical garden, which they had bought from this guy. It was a descendant of what I collected in the Himalayas." During a stroll through the Atlanta Botanical Garden's greenhouse the other day, we visited some of those Himalayan descendants, prompting a smile and a touch from Hauke.

Back in the 1960s, ten years before the Himalayan trip, Hauke went to Costa Rica, looking for the giant horsetail, brewed in a tea by some *campesinos* to treat kidney ailments. Growing to at least sixteen feet, the giant reed "is always a stirring sight," Hauke wrote in a science bulletin.

Not many people make a career of traveling the world looking for stirring sights, and Hauke, who was able to do this largely through research grants and sabbaticals, knows his good fortune. "When I was deciding to become a botanist," he said, "one of the reasons was this would give me the opportunity to travel. . . . Having come from a very humble background, I never had the wherewithal to go traveling."

He says his relationship with the horsetail reed began in graduate school at the University of Michigan in the 1950s, when he learned of "a good representation of horsetails" on a lake.

In studying this plant, he found there were few enough species to allow him to know them all in detail and that there was "a lack of competition" with other researchers. "There are people who have studied it at different times from different standpoints," he said, "but nobody has made that their main focus."

Joining the conversation, his wife, Kathleen, said he's always told her he studied horsetails simply because "somebody needed to do it." Then, she added, "He likes being the world's expert on it."

The couple, married since 1958 and the parents of four, have seen a lot of the world in the search for reeds. On some trips, she said, the family would pack themselves into a VW and "our eyes would be peeled, looking for equisetum. All our vacations were field trips."

May 13, 1994

PATIENT GARDENER? NOT ALWAYS

Amazing how a lazy, carefree outing can turn into a cross-country hunt that tries patience (mine) and inspires resourcefulness (somebody else's).

Here we were, about a dozen strong, rocking and rolling up the highway in one of those little luxury buses, on an idyllic spring garden trip organized by Wade Burns, neighbor, architect, gardener.

With a whole lot of junk food and sodas under our belts, we pulled into Greenwood, South Carolina, near lunchtime and wound our way to our destination: the remarkable garden of John Elsley, director of horticulture at Wayside Gardens, who formerly held posts at the St. Louis Botanical Garden and the Royal Horticultural Society Garden at Wisley, England.

Elsley's extensive travels, positions and contacts have helped him put his hands on some rare and wonderful plants, many of which are unavailable in the trade — including a showy black lenten rose, several Japanese maples and some hostas. All these and more drew oohs and aahs from Lyn and me, from longtime civic activists-gardeners Dan and Tally Sweat and the rest of our group.

As interesting as it was to see the many unusual trees, perennials and shrubs Elsley has collected in the fourteen years he's been building his Greenwood garden, the plant that spoke loudest to me was a relatively unrare Japanese hydrangea vine (Schizophragma hydrangeoides).

Clinging to an oak, the vine had climbed about fifty feet (several books say it goes to only thirty feet) and was filled with white blooms. At first I thought it was the same as the climbing hydrangeas that I've had on brick walls for years (Hydrangca petolaris), but a closer look showed that this one was different. The flower was showier, and the vine had thicker, coarser-toothed leaves. And Elsley pointed out that it blooms later than the climbing hydrangea.

I had to have it.

As it was not among Elsley's hard- or impossible-to-get plants, I figured that finding the vine would be an easy, peaceful venture. Wrong.

On the next day of business, I got on the telephone, which led to a flashback: A couple of years ago I wanted a Norfolk Island pine in June, only to be told by countless nursery folks that this was a "Christmas plant. Try us again in December."

Now, I was being told by one nursery after another, including Wayside, that they planned to offer the vine next spring. But not now. Too late.

I couldn't wait until next spring; patience doesn't last that long. Still dialing, I got around to Winterthur, in Delaware, where I had found a weeping dogwood. No, said the woman at the plant department, they didn't have the hydrangea vine, but she'd call around and see if she could help me locate it.

Believing that was the last I'd hear from her, I was trying to figure my next move (maybe talk ol' John Elsley out of a cutting). Then — it was no more than a day later — she called back, saying she'd located the plant at one of Winterthur's suppliers in Oregon, a nursery called Forestfarm.

Boom! I was on the phone again. Yes, said the voice from Forestfarm, they had some vines and would be happy to ship one. The news felt so good, you'd think I'd won the lottery.

The vine arrived in late May and was in the ground next to our tulip tree before you could say *Schizophragma hydrangeoides*.

Then I sat back on the front porch, looked at the tall, stately tree, with its gray, deeply grooved bark and imagined it hugged by the vine in full flower — an effect that Julie Harrod, in her book *The Garden Wall* describes as "dramatic, each flower-head measuring perhaps a foot across and making a good display after midsummer, for a longer period than the climbing hydrangea's brief fortnight."

At a mere foot or so in height, my plant has a long way to go. Ever since I planted it, I have stopped each day to urge it onward and upward. Grow. Climb that tree, I say silently.

Elsley said he put his in six or seven years ago. And in a recent conversation he spoke matter-of-factly about long waits on some plants' maturing and flowering, mentioning tree peonies as an example. "You have to have patience," he said.

Ummmm, yes. Patience. It certainly is a gardening staple. But patience also is a virtue that even gardeners sometimes lose.

September 23, 1994

PRIMEVAL WHISPERS

Savannah, Georgia — Bamboo sends me.

Its appeals are many, including its messages on the wind — messages that change with the seasons and with the air currents running through leaves and canes.

Sometimes bamboo whispers softly like a gentle spring breeze speaking peace and love and renewal. In a gale, it rustles, hoarse, dry, crackling like a fire or a rattler, signaling trouble ahead. Often it simply stands, offering mute testimony to the power of silence. And to the power of simple beauty.

That beauty and power, along with bamboo's airborne poetry, all draw me to it, to the dismay of some gardening friends who shun bamboo as invasive, likening it to the dread kudzu. "What do you water it with, used motor oil?" I've been asked.

Never mind. I love bamboo, actually inviting it to my garden. Now I'm up to about ten types, having gotten them from nurseries, mail-order catalogs, friends and deserted sites. I've planted black bamboo, golden, weeping, gray, dwarf, palm leaf — and some (gathered from a vacant lot in my neighborhood) with no name, at least no name I know.

My relationship with bamboo goes way, way back. Back to when I was growing up in Meridian, Mississippi, where we boys made whistles of canes cut alongside streams and my parents and I turned tall reeds into fishing poles. In fact, golden bamboo, one of the more common varieties, also is called fishpole bamboo. Apparently, we were not alone in saving money on fishing equipment.

All that history and love are about to be tested again. We are approaching the time of year when running bamboo, such as golden, will shoot new canes across my small garden, trying desperately to cover the entire space. "How do you keep it from taking over, shoot it?" inquiring friends want to know.

When the shoots (I've never cooked them, though I've loved them in Chinese restaurants) reach four or five inches, they are easily broken off and thrown in the trash can. Wary of a new, unwanted plant's rising like a sci-fi monster that regenerates from a single toe, I'd never put these broken shoots in my compost pile. If I miss any shoots — and that's easy to do because they emerge by the dozens — I reach for the pruning shears.

True, keeping the canes where I want them can be very time-consuming, but being able to look out my window and see and hear a stand of bamboo waving over a large stone makes it all worthwhile.

Such pleasure was multiplied countless times recently when I visited the bamboo farm about twelve miles south of Savannah, on U.S. 17.

Formerly and formally called the Coastal Area Extension Center, the farm, operated by the University of Georgia Cooperative Extension Service, is changing its name to the more descriptive Coastal Gardens, Historic Bamboo and Horticultural Collections.

The forty-six-acre farm, which is open to the public daily from sunrise to sunset, boasts dozens of species of crape myrtle, some not yet available in the trade, along with twenty types of holly, hundreds of types of roses, daylilies, hibiscus, herbs, perennials and annuals.

But the main attraction remains bamboo. At least for me, it does.

I found a kindred soul in Frank Linton, agricultural research assistant at the farm and a bamboo lover at heart. "It fascinates me," he says. "It's different, depending on whether it's in the rain, cold, heat. It's soothing. It's fun to be out here in it."

Lyn and I got out in it on a cool, drizzly day, arriving around noon at the farm, whose entrance has the biggest, tallest bamboo we'd ever seen: Japanese giant timber bamboo. Some of its canes measure three inches in diameter and reach fifty feet high. The grove, now covering an acre, began in 1890 as three little plants transplanted from a nearby estate to this spot, which then was a family farm.

That was the beginning of a collection that now includes some 165 varieties of bamboo, collected from temperate zones around the world and ranging from the huge timber bamboo to tiny fern types. Some plants are available for purchase.

Linton is working on a history of the facility, noting that Barbour Lathrop, a Chicago collector, bought the farm in 1919 and donated it to the federal government for use as a plant intro-duction garden. The garden evaluated foreign plants to deter-mine if they could be grown here and propagated for distribution to states suitable for their cultivation. Thousands of plants from the farm have been distributed throughout the United States, Linton says.

In 1983, the extension service began operating the farm, as the state acquired it from the federal government.

During the facility's lifetime, bamboo has been the object of unrealized American dreams, embodied in hopes that the canes would be widely used in construction and furniture making. Bamboo also has been the subject of ambitious studies, ranging from unsuccessful efforts to produce rubber from it to use of DNA from leaf samples to identify species. The DNA research is still going on.

Practicing what they preach, farm officials have installed fences of bamboo. Such ornamental garden uses for bamboo may represent this nation's most successful effort to make use of the plentiful canes.

Pandas certainly have done their part to use bamboo, feasting on leaves harvested at the farm and shipped to zoos. I've found that our cats are fond of the leaves, too.

Charles Bruce, farm director since 1983 (Linton began that year, too), says visits range from seven to ten thousand a year, including a lot of elementary school students, as well as members of garden and herb clubs.

In an effort to increase attendance, officials are trying to make the farm more noticeable from the highway. They are working on a new, catchier sign for the entrance, a sign Bruce promises will be graphically "state of the art," depicting maybe a hibiscus bloom or daylily. And bamboo.

A grove of bamboo is worth a thousand pictures.

We drove by grove after grove, enjoying spotted bamboo, golden, black, silver-gray, bamboo with swollen joints, some with swollen canes. (One swollen-cane type inspires my all-time favorite common name for a bamboo: Buddha's belly.) We saw bamboo that was tall, short, weeping, young, old. In large groves and small.

Out of the car, we walked inside several groves, including the giant timber one. The experience was wonderfully real and, at the same time, otherworldy. Permeated by mist, darkened by the close-growing canes, the grove was a forest, quiet, solitary, limitless.

"Primeval," Lyn called it. Indeed, this could have been a scene from eons ago. It was the ultimate outdoors, through the ages. Mist, mud, plants growing.

We marveled at the evocativeness of this simple setting, walking through it, touching the cool, smooth, hard canes, occasionally knocking together two large ones to hear their ancient "thock. Thock-thock," along with the rustle of leaves.

Then we stopped and listened to everything go silent. It was powerfully beautiful.

March 17, 1995

FOILED AGAIN

There's nothing like a squirrel. Bushy-tailed and energetic, one of these little creatures can provide endless entertainment as it scampers up and down a tree, dashing about the limbs. A mob of them, twirling, chasing, flying, looks like more fun than a kindle of kittens.

Looks can deceive.

There's nothing like a squirrel to undo the good you do in a garden.

Squirrels have done more to tick me off than any other garden pest I've encountered. More than slugs or snails. Or worms (not earthworms; they're good worms). More than beetles, aphids, whiteflies, scales or mites. Squirrels, which really are just bushy-tailed rats, are the worst.

Unfortunately, they are much like weather; most gardeners

talk about them but realize there's virtually nothing we can do about them. That hasn't stopped us from trying, though.

Recently, I heard about a birdseed coated with cayenne pepper, designed to burn the squirrels but not the birds. I don't buy seed for the birds, relying instead on plant seeds and berries to attract them. But the hot seed reminds me of the time I sprinkled pepper around young, weak little perennial plantings that squirrels so love to raid. With the pepper, I was hoping to make the varmints dance like a Western movie gunslinger dodging lead. Then there was the time I doused plant leaves with Tabasco, trying to set their mouths on fire.

A couple of years ago, after I heard of a California product using mountain-lion urine (I haven't a clue how they got it), I began spreading used cat litter around new plantings in my garden. Also, I've tried cat hair and human hair and cedar shavings.

Well, all of these worked for a hot minute. Then I'd go into the garden and see squirrels scampering away, flicking their tails profanely, leaving behind freshly dug holes — and plants.

Like a basement chemist hopelessly in love with the notion of one day discovering a magic potion, I continue seeking remedies to repel the arrogant rodents.

My latest effort developed after I had solved another problem around the house: gutters. Following their removal, I discovered that the troublesome, eternally leaf-clogged things' repeated overflowing had rotted even more wood than I had feared. Including a spot at the corner of the house that made an opening just big enough for a squirrel. A couple of the rodents immediately seized the opportunity and took up residence somewhere in the attic, above the kitchen.

A wood man repaired the spot and painted all around the edge of the now-gutterless house, leaving me with the nice knowledge that I wouldn't have to worry again about cleaning gutters a half dozen times a year. And — no small matter — I looked forward to sitting quietly in the kitchen without hearing scampering squirrels doing morning exercises and preparing to dash out to work. Life was improving.

The morning after the repairs, I heard the heart-sinking sound through the kitchen ceiling: Scratch, scratch. Scratch, scratch, scratch, followed by frantic dashing back and forth, then quiet.

The squirrel couple had been sealed in, inadvertently. They were racing around seeking a way out. Finding none, they apparently would stop to contemplate their plight and catch their breath. Should I undo the repair and watch the space until they were safely out, then reseal it?

A day or so later, before I could answer the question, I happened to look along the roofline on another part of the house, where I saw a brand-new hole, just chewed through — from the inside; the pair had escaped.

I moved quickly, buying a piece of sheet metal and a bunch of nails to cover the newly chewed hole. In the process, I got some free advice from the hardware-store man on how to make sure the squirrels wouldn't come back: Put mothballs in the hole, something I knew about, having scattered zillions of them through my garden because squirrels are supposed to hate the smell. I believe the mothballs became squirrel soccer balls.

The man's other suggestion was more promising. Sprinkle sulfur around the spot at the roofline, he said, asserting that squirrels can't stand it. I don't know whether they're supposed to hate inhaling it or whether it burns their raggedy little feet.

Hmmm. Why not sprinkle sulfur around plant containers and on the brickwork, too? I did. It seemed to work, as one day I saw a squirrel approach a sulfur-surrounded bonsai tray, newly planted with three trident maples.

The squirrel hopped to within a foot of the tray, stopped at the sulfur line, sniffed the air, twitched its tail, raised a paw as if to step forward, then turned and ran.

Amid my cheering, I had a sobering thought. Had I really won? The squirrel could go to some other garden and avoid my sulfur, but I had to stay around and smell its pollution of lovely fragrances: jasmine, wisteria, rose, banana shrub. The acrid-sweet smell reminded me of a childhood remedy for some long-forgotten ailment. Molasses and something.

I reached for the hose pipe. Foiled again. Swish. The sulfur was gone.

I hear garlic powder may be worth a try.

April 14, 1995

OVERALLS

After years of looking over the fancy pants in the gardening magazines — but never ordering any — I recently figured out the perfect garment for bending and reaching and digging and planting: overalls.

Amazing that it took me all these gardening decades to get a clue and decide to make this leap forward into the past. But then, sometimes the most obviously logical solutions are the ones we come to last. This is another case that recalls the saying I heard many times as a child (and quite a few as an adult): "If it had been a snake, it would've bit you."

Deciding to buy overalls was one thing; finding them was quite another.

I had been moving toward overalls for years, without knowing it: Back in the 1980s, I began wearing suspenders. In truth, I wore them more for fashion than for style or comfort. Somehow, suspenders (the word braces always makes me think of dentists) seemed right in that decade of smoke and mirrors, epitomized by the false fortunes won and lost in games of money, stocks, bonds and futures.

In the '80s, sleight of hand was everywhere. On presidential campaigns I covered in 1984, for example, twenty-five-year-old reporters passed themselves off as experienced simply by pulling on suspenders, smoking cigars and spouting political buzzwords.

By the time I got to the 1990s, I had discovered the real value of suspenders, having lived half a century and having grown as big around the middle as many of the pols I wrote about.

Fashion aside, suspenders are just plain comfortable. Good thing this discovery wasn't a snake.

A small problem: My suspenders are the kind you hook onto buttons inside waistbands, so I couldn't use them on my raggedy old gardening trousers. Thus, I had to leave my suspender comfort at the garden gate.

It wasn't until I got to know my father (we got together six years ago after being estranged for thirty-nine) that I began thinking of moving into gardening overalls for their loose, comfortable fit.

The first time I visited my father at his home in Meridian, Mississippi, he was wearing a pair of deep-blue bib overalls (or overhalls, as some of my relatives used to call them). On subsequent visits since that first in 1989, those overalls have grown bigger and bigger, as my father shrank into illness and old age. His once-lush garden is no more, but he continues to wear his overalls, inspiring in me a mixture of admiration for his unwavering style and sadness at his shrinking. I smile once in a while when I think how fashionable he would be in the hip-hop world of baggier-than-thou pants.

Knowing that a man who knows so much about gardening certainly knows what's best to wear, I decided a couple of months ago to buy a couple of pairs of overalls. Seemed an easy enough plan to carry out. It wasn't.

I began by telephoning the stores I thought likely to sell work clothes, stores that used to send out thick "wish books." Yes, said salespeople at several places, they had overalls. However, the sizes they had in stock all seemed made for very short, very wide men, making me wonder if buyers believed that a whole lot of overalls wearers are five-by-five (five feet tall, five feet wide). I often feel that wide, but I'm a foot taller.

At one point in my search, driving to Meridian for Father's Day, I stopped in York, Alabama, a town small enough to sell overalls, I figured. I figured wrong. In the first store I visited, several women working there just stared when I asked about overalls. Finally, one said, "Nobody wears 'em anymore. 'Cept the kids."

To be sure, we've bought several pairs of overalls for grandchildren in the past several years. And the other day I received a picture of my very stylish daughter, Petria, wearing a pair of bib overalls. Wait a minute. What's wrong with this picture? Petria, who lives in New York and sometimes Europe, doesn't even garden.

At another store in York, a young, chuckling clerk said, "Overalls? No, I've never seen them in the store." And two old men sitting on a shaded bench near the main street said they hadn't seen anyone selling overalls in town since they couldn't remember when.

Frustrated, I broke down and decided to go to one of those young stores in Atlanta, the kind brimming with all kinds of denim but also jumping with noise masquerading as music. Picking my way through the tight, tight jeans, through the loose-fit jeans that also were tight, I found a pleasant surprise: overalls.

True, they are preshrunk and prefaded, not the true-blue kind I remember from childhood — and know from my father. Not the kind made for hard work on houses or in fields. Or gardens. But at least they aren't yellow. Or red. They're light blue, 100 percent cotton, soft and, most important, real big. Gardening in them is a joyful ease.

In some ways, buying these fancy overalls was like buying a fashionable new hybrid plant instead of the hardy old native I might prefer. I know my father would never be caught in overalls like this. They're a bit too young. Too fresh. But I can live with them. Until the real thing comes along.

July 14, 1995

STALKING ROSEMARY

The ritual went on for months, beginning sometime in January. I'd hop into the car, dash onto I-75 south and zip out to the State Farmer's Market. There, I'd drive to the group of vendor sheds off to the left — those displaying plants and trees.

Down at the end of one of the mostly empty sheds, where herbs and flowers had been sold last summer, I'd ogle the object of my desire: a rosemary about eighteen inches tall, in a red-clay-colored plastic pot. Alas, I couldn't have it. Its owner wasn't around.

Each trip, I could feel these words from a blues song: "I got my eyes on you." I was caught up in the chase. Lusting after the unattainable has a way of raising its value. We've all been there — one way or another. You set your eyes and heart on something and hope that when you finally get it, the reality will be as fine as the dream.

The first time ever I saw the aromatic shrub, I wanted it because of its shape. Its one-inch trunk curved upward, spawning branches that looked like pleats in an elegant silk fan.

That first day, I got out of my car and looked at the rosemary from all sides. I brushed it, releasing that smell that always arouses my appetite. I looked around for somebody to take my money. I was ready to buy.

But because it was off-season, only a few vendors were out, and none knew how much the owner wanted.

I thought briefly of stuffing the shrub into the trunk of my car and leaving a calling card with a note, then dismissed the idea. I drove away, hungry, empty-trunked.

When one of our countless false springs arrived, I went back. A few more vendors had opened for business, but not the one I was looking for.

By March, I was circling the rosemary every weekend. Now, I wanted it not only for its shape; watching it remain alive through one killer cold after another convinced me this was one tough rosemary. Certainly tougher than the three I had seen die in my garden.

I kept my eyes on it, and, I suspect, the market's security guards kept their eyes on me as I checked on the plant each Saturday or Sunday afternoon.

On April 13 I got my satisfaction.

Peggy Mattox of Griffin, the owner, had returned. She listened patiently as I recounted my calls on this plant I had to have. Seems she had been at the market occasionally since I first spied the rosemary but never during my visits. Yet, again, timing's everything.

Mattox didn't seem too keen on letting go of the plant — Tuscan Blue, she said — but did so anyway, playing angel to my merciless craving. My eyes, still on the prize, had turned absolutely van Gogh-ish, I'm sure.

As I picked out a few herbs and marigolds, Mattox mentioned surveillances similar to mine that she and other plant sellers have undertaken: watching plants under stress to see how they fared and to determine if they were worth buying and selling. You never know who's watching what.

We chatted a bit more and said good-bye as I promised to treat the rosemary right.

I let it stay in its old home for almost a week before repotting it, not wanting to take it through too many changes too soon.

So far, so good.

The rosemary, showing new growth, reaches out into a walkway on the side of the house, brushing all who pass, pungently acknowledging us.

The chase is over, the pursued ensconced. And to my relief and delight, it looks and feels as good at home as it did out there, in the marketplace.

April 27, 1996

PASSION'S THE THING

At Fernbank Science Center the other day, as staff members and I were chatting about gardening and life, passions and pastimes, Rachel Fiore posed an intriguing question: Can you learn to love gardening? The group, which included a wealth of expert and dedicated gardeners like my friend Sally Hodges, buzzed with interest, and I think most of us believed the answer was no, you can't make love happen.

Later, Rachel expanded on her question, noting that she was "not worried about whether I have a green thumb," adding that, "It seems to me that a true gardener just loves the gardening more than the product." For her part, Rachel loves flowers and plants, loves walking among them, but, she says, "I wonder if I am missing a great pleasure that would give me a sense of calm or connection, or if I am destined to get that feeling (in) other ways."

Having watched her mother and husband garden, it's understandable that Rachel would wonder what she's missing. The fact is, however, gardening is not for everyone. At least, not in every stage of life.

That's especially important to remember this time of year in Atlanta, when spring is clearing its throat, trying to nudge winter off the stage. This week, when I stood on my back porch and enjoyed the Carolina jessamine's twirling to the top of the saucer magnolia, breathing in their mingling sweetnesses, I felt profoundly the power of gardening's seductive call.

At the same time, I understood that some cannot heed the call.

I am always happy to talk with and receive mail from people who start off by saying, "I don't garden, but I read your column." While gardening has given me many fun-making and life-changing relationships, it is also true that some of my best friends, including my wife, are nongardeners. In fact, Lyn's aversion to putting trowel to earth has earned her the handle, She Who Appreciates But Does Not Garden.

And appreciating is one of the more important aspects of gardening — whether done by the gardener or someone else.

Moreover, other pastimes can enthrall. Golf, antiquing, fly-fishing, quilting can bring pleasures that, for some, must be akin to what I feel for gardening.

Knowing that, I do not proselytize. Although I get a kick out of sharing passions with those I love and like, I understand that shared experiences do not necessarily include having others get dirt under their fingernails. If you really stretch the point about gardening being done at any speed, you can argue that appreciating is gardening of a sort.

In fact, for some, there's no need to go beyond appreciating. And perhaps no payoff, either. You shouldn't dig and plant and water unless you really feel it. Passion is the most important gardening tool you'll ever use. Without it, the pain that gardening can bring just may not be worth tolerating.

So it was on the one occasion that Lyn decided to help me garden. About ten years ago, she watered indoor plants while I was traveling. When I got back home, I saw that sad sight — several cacti, swollen, brown and mushy, sprawled across the sand like bloated porcupines.

The killed cacti were not nearly as important as Lyn's hurt at having done them in, apparently by drowning. Lyn has not watered for me again — even though she keeps her office plants going just fine. No cacti, though.

And no watering any plants at home. No digging and planting and pruning, either. Maybe Lyn will one day love all that, but I think she shouldn't. Partly because, yes, I enjoy hogging gardening's pleasures. And partly because one addict in the house is quite enough.

March 8, 1997

MAGNIFICENT OBSESSION

Because Leslie Breland works so many after-dark hours in her northeast Atlanta garden, her sister threatened to buy her a miner's helmet to light up the night.

Chuckling at the image, Breland acknowledged it might not be such a bad idea: "I've been known to come out here at midnight with a flashlight, planting, pulling up weeds — I refuse to step over a weed — deadheading, pruning, cutting flowers. With the helmet, I could have both hands free."

This is what it has come to. It all started with a few roses and a hydrangea in early 1994, when Breland began gardening at her Morningside neighborhood home after a traumatic divorce. A few shrubs grew into a great big garden whose hundreds of plants amount to a wonderful tonic for the eyes, nose and soul. So proud is Breland that she carries pictures of her garden's stages, just as parents show off images of their children at various ages.

What you see in the pictures is how a once-empty space fills in more and more with shrubs, trees, perennials, a pond, pergola, gazebo, bridge, paths — while the grass space shrinks. (Individual plants mirror the transformation; a butterfly bush Breland bought as a skinny foot-long baby two years ago now is taller, broader than a man.) What you also see is a powerful example of how gardeners progress through three main stages: pastime, passion and, finally, obsession. It is a magnificent obsession.

"Every minute I have free, I'm out there," Breland says, noting that she did all the planting and some of the construction, including installing the pond, terracing, building a footpath of boards. Her obvious elegance is backed by surprising muscle.

Her work pays off in stunning fashion. Cutting a lovely bouquet, Breland gathered big, lush butterfly blooms, calla lily, daylily, hydrangea, rose, settling them into an arrangement recalling an Impressionist painting. She's up to 138 rose bushes now and grows, among others, gardenia, monarda, rose of Sharon, azalea, hollyhock. Breland's garden, with its many seating areas providing varying points of view, begs for outdoor parties.

So much time in the garden teaches Breland much. Resilience, for example. And strength: "No matter how much manure drops on you, the beauty rises through. Strongly."

All of us who've crossed the line from passion to obsession know the telltale signs. My car cannot pass a nursery without wheeling in. Returning from a trip, I always stop to visit with my family of plants. Communing turns to weeding, pruning; before I know it, I've been gardening for hours, tired no more. Neither heat, nor cold, nor rain nor hunger nor dark of night keeps the obsessed from working our appointed grounds.

Last fall, the stylish native New Yorker's shopping patterns offered graphic proof of her crossover: "I knew something had changed when I stopped making Lord & Taylor my very first stop. Home Depot and Pike — those are my shopping stops now."

Around Mother's Day, Breland's stepfather casually pointed

out that the above-ground pond she had put in would look a lot better in a spot ten feet away. "I agreed and started moving it before he and my mother left," Breland recalled as we walked through her garden the other day, enjoying the cool drizzle.

How did she get this way?

"I saw how beautiful those first few rose bushes were, and I wanted more. More. More." The resulting "lushness, pride, sense of accomplishment, the sheer beauty" continue to drive her need for more.

Breland may garden through the day and into the night, but at times she enjoys, too. Her contemplative appreciation is the counterpoint to her tireless work: "Sometimes I'll literally come home, drop my briefcase and sit in the swing in this pergola and just look out on nature and God and beauty. I say my blessings every day in the garden."

The pleasure of just looking and the pleasure taken in garden work constantly confront each other. This summer, Breland is vowing to "not always feel I've got to do and fix and improve. I really want to see if I can just come out and get a book and enjoy it. Sit and read, listen to music. But I'm wondering if I can really do that without seeing another patch that can be cultivated."

No. Later, during our stroll, as she pointed out "uncharted territory" on her property, visions of new plants danced in her eyes. More.

May 9, 1997

HUNTING ELDERBERRY

Barbara Johnston of Norcross is on a quest. Elderberry is what she's after. She's seen the berried shrub growing wild alongside the road, but it's been unreachable. And her chance of finding it in plant nurseries is about as good as finding prickly pear cactus.

Like many of us who fix on a plant, Johnston is seeking something beyond the shrub; she's looking for sweet times associated with elderberry. In an e-mail chat, she explained that, several Octobers ago she and her aunt in California had driven to a spot on a forest road in the mountains where her uncle had been chopping wood. There, elderberry bushes were blooming and berrying at the same time.

"This worked out beautifully," Johnston recalls. "She battered and fried the blooms, then we ate them with the wonderful compote she made from the berries.

"I know this is one of those special memories I can't duplicate and probably shouldn't mess with, but I just know that having my own bush is going to be a great reminder of that special time we all spent together."

So many memories grow out of plants. Most gardeners have grown or known some tree, shrub, perennial, houseplant that connects them to a person or place, evoking special images, fond recollections.

These plants that trigger memories seem rarely to be rare plants. Or expensive ones. Those I often hear and think about are so common, in fact, that nurseries usually don't stock them — either believing they are easy enough to find in the wild or just plain unworthy.

Mimosa, for example, speaks to legions of us who, as children, climbed these trees, brushing their ferny leaves, picking their pink powder-puff blossoms, sometimes sucking the nectar from them — always marveling at how their leaves close in rain and darkness, always appreciating their magical embrace.

Then there's prickly pear, the wonderful hardy cactus that

beckons from yards all across the South, spiny, sometimes upright, sometimes sprawling, blooming big and yellow in spring and summer — flowers that are followed by fruit used in Mexican food. It was its exotic nature that resonated with me as a child; to see cactus climbing from used automobile tires painted white in the Mississippi winter was my Southern substitute for the saguaro giants of Arizona.

And chinaberry holds priceless memories for generations of former boys and girls who used the hard little berries as ammunition in slingshots and for necklaces of green pearls that ripened to yellow. The experts always praise the fragrance of chinaberry's blossoms but warn of the ripe berries' odor. Funny, that smell never bothered any kid I knew.

Barbara Johnston's elusive elderberry provided the raw material for the popguns we boys made, cutting a foot of wild elderberry cane and pushing out its pithy center with a wire coat hanger.

Not all my memory-bearing plants are as difficult to find for sale as elderberry. Browsing through the Georgia Agriculture Department's Farmers and Consumers Market Bulletin unearths mullein, elephant ears, morning glory, four o'clock. They, and many other good old-timey plants grow out of the bulletin's pages, taking me way back to Big Momma's Alabama garden.

It was country, and now it would be cool; many of those old plants are in vogue. Look at the popularity zinnia is enjoying. And cabbage, grown for show, is tres chic these days. Big Momma would get a kick out of that.

So, I hope Barbara Johnston doesn't give up the hunt for elderberry. Even if she can't dig any out of the wild, she just might find it someday soon at an enterprising nursery — right next to the sweet shrub.

November 29, 1997

Willow-leaf fig

Ficus · salicifolia

PART THREE

PEOPLE

Look at a garden,
see the gardener

~

BONSAI FEVER

SNIP. SNIP-SNIP.

That's the sound of Andrew Young, clipping dead needles off a prized pine, dwarfed and displayed in an earth-colored tray. It is a sound heard too seldom, he says.

Snip. "I really am embarrassed that I don't do more with them," he says, clipping and caressing the plant, then gesturing to about a dozen more that sit waiting on his wooden deck in southwest Atlanta. "About all I get to do is water them."

Andrew Young has a growing problem.

For about five years, he has been in the grip of bonsai fever, gathering the dwarfed ornamental trees from a variety of sources. But pruning roots and branches to keep them small, watering, repotting and simply appreciating his collection can take huge chunks of time.

And, if you know anything about Andy Young, you know that a lot of free time is what he doesn't have.

A top official at the Atlanta Committee for the Olympic Games and at Law International Inc., an engineering and environmental consulting firm, Young remains a dedicated rights activist worldwide. His résumé includes positions as an aide to Dr. Martin Luther King Jr., as a U.S. congressman (elected three times), as U.S. ambassador to the United Nations and as mayor of Atlanta (two terms).

In short, he's a very busy man who goes a lot.

For a traveling man, bonsai can be tough to cultivate. Like children, the trees grow amazingly fast when you're away, making you feel a keen sense of time lost. And when you return, you work hard to make up for the absence.

Young's problem is a struggle between two passions: one an absorbingly educational pastime, the other a burning need to work and to do good works. It is a struggle that increasingly resonates with people who, like Young, have had rewarding careers, then discovered rewarding hobbies at a time when many their age are contemplating retirement. In bonsai and Young, we have a very private pastime for an exceedingly public person.

As he prunes and grooms, Young, in a colorful jogging suit and athletic shoes, likens his love of the trees in shallow trays to "an addiction," but makes it clear that he's holding the addiction in check. For now.

Always a man from whom you should expect the unexpected, Young knocks down the traditional view of bonsai collectors as Zen-like people who have found eternal peace through miniaturized trees.

"I've learned that I'm still too restless for this hobby," he says with a laugh (when we talked recently, he was just back from a trip to Africa centering on business and voter-education meetings, and he was preparing to travel to New York). "This hobby is for somebody with a lot more time and patience than me."

Bonsai growing, he says, is "sort of like setting aside a hobby for a later date. I can water them and let them grow wild and pinch them back occasionally, and then whenever I do have time, I've got something I can work with."

Noting that it takes many years to train a bonsai into a small version of a tree in nature, weathered and windswept, Young says: "This is the hobby that I think I want to pursue seriously in retirement. But you don't wait until you're seventy-five to start gathering trees."

Starting his collection before retirement eliminates "the twig stage" of his hobby, he says. At sixty-one, he shows no signs of retiring, so his collection should be well aged by the time he sits down.

How long before that happens?

"I don't know. I keep thinking my life's going to slow down. I thought it would slow down when I left politics. But then we got the Olympics."

Until he slows down, Young tends when he can, and he learns all the time.

Bonsai, like the paintings and other art he and his wife, Jean, have collected over the years, have made him acutely aware of differing facets in his personality. The plants, which often mirror natural serenity, "show you how much you need calm," he says. "I need the calm, but I have to work out physically, too." Among his physical stress-busters are swimming and bicycling.

His plants, with their requirements for watering, feeding and grooming, "put a kind of routine into your life," he says. "You can't get so self-centered that you only think about yourself."

Travel destroys routine, he notes. "I get terribly lonely in a hotel room because I don't have things to do. Everything is done for you. Riding on a plane — everything is done for you. You need some things to do. Some connections to reality." And what is more real than a tree, a rock, a tray of soil?

Sometimes the knowledge reveals contradiction. He says, "I'm learning to appreciate simplicity," but, like many who collect something with passion, he latches onto so many plants that the simplicity is lost in the numbers.

In addition to his frequent trips to nurseries in search of "scraggly plants" that could be trained, Young was bringing in so many plants during his foreign travels that whenever customs officials saw him approach, they'd ask if he had any. He'd contact the U.S. Department of Agriculture in advance if he thought he'd be bringing in more booty.

How did he get this way?

It all began back in 1988, when, nearing the end of his second term as mayor of Atlanta, Young was given a bonsai, a juniper, by a local nursery official. He still has it.

That same year he made his first purchase, a boxwood, and later, while attending the Seoul Olympics, saw a bonsai exhibit in connection with the Games. He was so taken with the trees, Young left the horticulturist for the city of Seoul five hundred dollars and a request to send as many plants as that sum would buy.

He did pretty well, receiving seven plants, including a pine and a quince, both more than two feet tall now, with extremely well-developed trunks.

The shipment gave the novice collector a scare. Shipped not in pots, the trees "had been stripped completely," Young recalls. "They washed the roots and packed them in peat moss. I had just a few little strange sticks." He took them to a local bonsai expert, who helped him set them up in trays.

The former mayor has come a long way from those days. Since then, he has done bonsai business with Brother Paul, bonsai grower emeritus at the Holy Spirit Monastery in Conyers, who says Young always "knew pretty well what he wanted. He'd pick it out and take it. By the time he got to us, he was well versed" in the art of bonsai.

And, like all of us bonsai growers, he has kept enough trees thriving to feel some confidence, and he has buried enough to remain humble.

Young's interest in bonsai came just after Delta Air Lines and Japan Airlines established passenger routes between Atlanta and Tokyo and as Southerners were gaining heightened awareness of Japanese businesses and culture.

As mayor of the South's unofficial capital city, Young says he figured that because the city was attracting ever more Japanese businesses, and "if the destinies of the United States and Japan were going to be intertwined for at least the rest of my life, I needed to try to understand something of what it is about their lifestyle that has made them so successful."

He is still working on that. And, although he laments his lack of time for bonsai, he, his family and friends all agree he has reaped a lot of personal satisfaction from the hobby.

Carol Muldawer, a longtime associate and family friend — she was his administrative assistant in the mayor's office — said beginning the pastime "had a very calming, relaxing effect" on Young during stressful times. "When you're tending bonsai plants you really can't think about anything else but what you're doing."

For many years Andy Young was an unlikely bonsai man.

In fact, his childhood in New Orleans turned him off from growing practically anything. One of his chores was to dig drainage ditches to handle excess water in his father's rose garden. Another was going once or twice each year to somebody's cow pasture to collect fertilizer for the family compost heap.

Now Young is clearly a man in the grip of bonsai pleasure. And even as he asserts he has not yet learned patience, he demonstrates it.

He has waited for weeks for an apparently dead plant to show signs of life. A stand of miniature maples is becoming a forest as he watches. It could take years.

We talk about whether he should prune away a branch on his first bonsai, the juniper. I say yes because it grows in an opposite direction from the part of the plant that cascades. He says maybe, or maybe he'll wait for the smaller branch to grow long enough to cascade too. In bonsai, as in any other art form, what is "right" is in the eye of the beholder.

Although each bonsai is unique, all contribute to life's framework. For Young, this is a vital attribute.

Watering, pruning. Snip. Snip. "Those little simple routines do something for your life," says Young, wielding a small pair of pruners. "It's like feeding the dog, taking out the garbage. It provides a certain basic routine, along with brushing your teeth, combing your hair, taking your shower. That helps keep you sane."

An ordained minister who has pastored churches in Marion, Alabama, and in Thomasville and Beachton, Georgia, Young continues, saying, "We normally develop a pattern that meets our spiritual and emotional needs, as well as our physical needs.

"I don't think you could survive without it. That's civilization."

April 7, 1993

PLANT PEOPLE

The way some plants look and act can come in handy as a way of describing people.

She's as durable as pothos, for example. He wilts like a peace lily or rhododendron. What's up with Miss Thing? She's prickly as a cactus. They're a stately couple, solid, like an oak.

My list of possibilities is endless fun; it's always interesting and gratifying to find ways of linking plants and people.

For my part, this endeavor usually relies on ornamental plants to make a point or a description.

But Herman Smith, a long-time education official who most recently was coaxed out of retirement to serve as interim president of Morris Brown College, has developed a lively system in which people are compared to vegetables — to describe their work habits and productivity. Or lack of same.

Smith's fertile grounds in southwest Atlanta are the perfect setting to inspire such theorizing.

During a recent visit, we walked by his impatiens, salvia, zinnias, geraniums, roses and petunias, all of which were lovingly tended. And as we passed the morning glory, Smith gave one of its blooms a squeeze until it popped like those he remembered from childhood in Knoxville.

But our real destination was the vegetable garden, a plot that measures some forty-by-ninety feet. Of course, his is not just an organic vegetable garden; it's a collection of archetypes, because "people are just like vegetables."

Some types:

• Purple-hull peas. Smith says the plants "do not require a lot of attention. They're very tough, and they're prolific. Some people are like that." Accordingly, Purple-Hull Pea People "are very productive. They're almost self-starters." (Smith says pole beans "are right next to purple-hull peas.")

• Tomato (it's technically a fruit, you say. Let's include it because it has a veggie attitude). "They don't require much attention," Smith says of tomato plants and people. "They're beautiful to work with. Most rewarding. Very, very nice, and they just keep on producing." As his were on the day I visited.

• Okra. The plants "are slow getting started," Smith says, "but you just water them and take care of them, and when they feel like it, they will make you proud." While tough, they "need a lot of sunshine."

As for Okra People, "You have to give them everything they need and want. They have to have the desk that's big enough. And you have to give them the kind of pencils they like. They need two or three kinds of paper. If you provide all that, they'll produce, too. The Purple-Hull People don't have to have all that."

• Squash. Noting the overwhelming amounts of vines and leaves in relationship to the amount of squash produced, Smith says, "They're loquacious. They know everything. They run their mouths, and they produce very little."

This veggie-people system, which could be called "Smith's Hierarchy of Seeds," is part of his overall philosophy of gardening and education. He uses the pastime in much the way many of us do — as a stress buster — but also as a way of warding off Ivory Toweritis, a condition that afflicts academicians the world over.

Gardening "helps you remain down to Earth and in the real world," says Smith, who stepped down from his interim presidency to make way for Samuel Jolley, the new president of Morris Brown.

Smith not only uses the fruit of his gardening labor to describe people, he uses it to charm them, too.

Take tomatoes. That's exactly what he did at the Peachtree Kiwanis Club when he made a speech to the group back in July.

Smith's description is mouthwatering: "two large, freshly picked red tomatoes with slivers of green." He wrapped them in foil, the dew still on them.

When he got up to speak, he presented the tomatoes to Ray Nixon, the Kiwanis president. Smith recalls saying, "I am an incurable but productive gardener. It's nice to bring Exhibit A with me. I brought it to present to your president."

Ceremoniously unwrapping the foil, he said, "You see, you don't have to wonder whether I am a productive gardener.

"Now I would like to announce to the entire assemblage that I can talk to you this morning about gardening or about Morris Brown College, whichever you prefer."

The crowd loved it.

Nixon praised the tomatoes the other day, adding that he thought Smith was pretty swell, too.

"He's a terrific philosopher, a great observer of human nature." His comparisons of people to vegetables "make a lot of sense," says Nixon, a manager at Georgia Power.

"Everything in nature tends to follow some kind of pattern,"

Nixon says. "There are plants that are basically parasites, and people who are basically parasites. He's right on."

Okay, but what kind of vegetable is Smith?

"He's a tomato," Nixon says without hesitation. "No question about it, he's a producer."

October 15, 1993

"GARDENING KEEPS YOU YOUNG"

Leila Denmark, a pediatrician, has tended to children for sixty-six years. She has gardened since she was a youngster. At ninety-six, she has done enough of both to know that growing a child and growing a flower are alike in at least one important way.

"They both need a lot of attention," she told me recently, as we walked through her garden in Alpharetta.

A small woman with an engaging smile, Denmark is both gentle and fiery, delicately caressing her flowers, as she does her little patients, but always ready to rail against anything and anyone who does not nurture children.

Dr. Leila, as she is known, gives a great deal of attention to the growing spaces around her white-columned home and does everything she can to encourage parents to do the same for their children.

With the help of her seventy-three-year-old niece, Wilma Cravey, Denmark has developed a delightful plot in the back that includes roses, impatiens and zinnias. A river of hostas runs along the back of the house. A birdbath and a birdhouse share the space. Fittingly, Denmark views this picture-perfect space each morning from her breakfast table, through a wide-angle window. A pair of binoculars sits on the table, at the ready.

"I put food out for the birds, come back in and eat breakfast and watch the birds," she said. "It really works."

Of course, it cannot be proved that her calm, grace and longevity are attributable to gardening or to her extraordinary career in taking care of children. But I certainly believe that Dr. Leila gets something from both of them that supples her body and feeds her soul. Doing work that you love has to count for something. And doing gardening on top of that counts for something more.

I believed her when she told me, "Gardening keeps you young." And I know from experience that she is right in saying, "If you want to be happy, you have to do what you want to do."

No matter how impassioned you are about your work, you need a counterpoint to it. For Denmark, gardening, along with sewing, provides that counterpoint (she makes her own clothes). "You've got to have some recreation," she said.

The doctor gardens with the same fervor she demonstrates in her work to save children: lugging plants, deadheading blooms, spreading mulch. All around the house are beautiful signs of her recreation — hydrangeas, phlox, daylilies, hardy begonia, daphne. Her plants are happy, her beds neat and clean.

Before nine o'clock last Saturday morning, she was ebullient, recounting how she had begun her day. "I've been out there, pulling out weeds and grass," she said. "I planted some impatiens, too.

"You've got to have some exercise."

Moreover, she said, "Gardening is a part of me."

To be sure, the doctor has the gardening gene. She speaks fondly of her mother's flower garden in her native Portal, Georgia — particularly the roses, which seemed to need less care than those today. These days, she said, "You have to keep fooling with them." Her mother's must have been "the old-fashioned ones," she reasoned.

She may like old-fashioned roses, but Denmark roundly rejects what she says is generally old behavior.

"Most people, when they get older, go on tours, cruises and stuff, and get fat and eat themselves to death," she said. But not her.

The lithe doctor's diet sounds spare but not spartan. For breakfast she usually has an egg, cooked any way, whole-wheat toast, half a banana and water. No coffee. Right, no coffee. Lunch is lean meat, usually beef, two vegetables, bread and water. Dinner, she said, is the same as lunch.

Instead of touring and cruising, the doctor doctors a full work week, seeing patients from 8:00 A.M. "until we finish." Such hard work has been going on a very long time. At Atlanta's Egleston Children's Hospital, she was the first medical intern, in 1928.

So many years of doctoring have, of course, made her known to many as a pediatrician. But beyond that, Denmark has developed a reputation and drawn admiration for her joy of life and sense of adventure.

Julie Herron of the Atlanta Botanical Garden, who grew up in Sandy Springs, an Atlanta suburb, and knew of Dr. Leila, said the other day that she wouldn't be surprised to hear that the doctor was taking up, say, skydiving: "She's so accomplished, a great believer in continuing to learn and to stretch yourself."

When I passed on Herron's comment, Denmark had a quick response, noting that she learned to swim at age sixty-one. That was during a Caribbean cruise, she said, chuckling. She borrowed a bathing suit from her daughter and hit the water.

In gardening, too, the doctor stretches herself and her plants' limits. She is growing hydrangeas that came from the high ground of Highlands, North Carolina, and she defies conventional wisdom in getting good blooms from roses with soggy feet.

With the end of her swimming story still hanging in the misty morning air, Denmark led the way from the garden to her office, in a 130-year-old white farmhouse near her residence. Inside the little frame building, there was a stillness the other day, a Thursday, her day off unless somebody telephones with an emergency. The scales for weighing babies sat, unmoving, nestling only a tiny pastel blanket. On Denmark's desk, scores of pictures of little patients smiled through a glass cover. Similarly, a screen in the hallway displayed more pictures.

From time to time, the doctor said, patients and parents look across the way, see her blueberry bushes, her flowers in bloom, and ask for a closer look. It is likely, however, that many do not know how much work she puts into gardening; that is something she is not given to talking about.

For one thing, when she is with patients, she is taking care of business, trying to find out what is wrong and how to make it right. For another, I suspect that gardening remains a private part of her, albeit a distinctly passionate part. Like many achievers in all walks of life, she gets her chief pleasure from just doing it.

"Sometimes, when I come by, she's right there, down on her knees, digging the holes," Wilma Cravey said. "She has a tremendous amount of energy. If she ever has an ache or pain, you never hear about it."

Cravey called her aunt "an inspiration to me. She wants to help everything to live."

Precisely. Said Denmark, "I try to build flowers and build babies. That's life."

July 8, 1994

A SUSTAINING LOVE AFFAIR

Linda Wish and I met several years ago when I answered her advertisement for Japanese maples in the *Farmers and Consumers Market Bulletin*. She was selling, and I bought every chance I got.

Since then, we have kept in touch, loosely, talking about the law, her profession, writing, mine. And gardening, a passion for us both. Like me, Linda always has gardened indoors as avidly as outdoors. Lately, however, she's had a radical change of crops.

She is selling off her huge collection of long-tended indoor plants, such as Christmas cactus, peace lily, philodendron, amaryllis, China doll and many others. In their places, she has begun growing one type of plant: orchids.

Linda has a simple but profound explanation for the shift: chronic fatigue syndrome, also known as chronic fatigue and immune dysfunction syndrome, the illness that saps both physical and mental energy mercilessly and unpredictably. "For years, I grew fast-growing plants" that required constant attention, she explains. "Now I'm growing orchids. They're more my speed." She notes that orchids don't require pruning, rarely need repotting, "and they don't mind if you don't water them for a few days."

Also, of course, they're wickedly beautiful, and their blooms remain lovely, intriguingly sensual, for a long while.

Orchids' many attributes are not lost on others across the country; love for the plants keeps growing and growing and growing.

As a measure of their popularity, orchids, like bonsai, increasingly have followed more traditional houseplants into hardware stores, supermarkets and discount houses. And, as an example of their place on the cutting edge, orchids are growing topical on the information superhighway, say computing gardeners.

Like so much in gardening, orchids addict.

Linda certainly is proof of that. In some ways, her change of gardening is an accelerated version of what we all do over time. We slow down, find a groove that works for us. One of the joys of gardening is that it can be done at any speed — from the frenzied buying, digging and planting of newly landed gents and ladies bent on quickly transforming their bare lots into lush paradises to the stately pace of less able people, fragile through illness or age, who do little more than water, prune or just pet beloved plants.

It is one thing to feel your strength ebbing slowly, naturally. It is quite another to feel it bolt away like a wild horse. That is the way it went for Linda, who is forty-five. Harvard educated, a successful corporate lawyer since 1973, she had almost never taken sick time from work. She had exercised regularly. Then, in 1991, she noticed that aerobics became more and more difficult.

"When I did the warm-ups, I got colder," she recalls. "I knew something was wrong."

Fatigue became a way of life. Cognitive problems struck, too. Reading with comprehension became virtually impossible, a critical blow to a lawyer's career. Driving in traffic became tough. Her handwriting deteriorated (she'd write an "m," and it'd have four or five humps, for example). She says she'd talk to someone needing something, do it in five minutes, then forget who had needed it. Of her lack of stamina, she says, "I can do anything for a short period of time, but I deteriorate quickly."

Reflecting life in a litigious society as well as the extent of her incapacitation, Linda says, "I became afraid I was going to mess up" and get sued.

Unable to work now, she fights the mysterious, controversial illness (some doctors still assert it's only in the mind) with vitamins, food supplements, seven prescription drugs and two support groups. And orchids.

Recently, I visited Linda's north Atlanta home to see how her gardening change was coming along. Her speech had slowed a bit, but her sense of humor had not. "I basically live on this sofa," she said from a reclining position. She recounts a friend's comparing her to "a lump of butter on a hot August afternoon," slumping and melting.

Ah, but the dozens of orchids near a living room window seem to strengthen her, emotionally if not physically, though I can never know what price she paid later for her enthusiasm.

Linda explains that she took up orchid growing in earnest about a year ago after a few unsuccessful forays. Now she grows zillions. Throughout the house where other houseplants used to live, orchids bloom white, yellow, violet, mottled, looking like everything from butterflies to birds in flight.

In the basement she has hundreds more, under fluorescent lights, many recently situated in the places where other houseplants used to reign. "I find, on average, at least one bud a day," she boasts, reminding me that I have grown several orchids for years, rarely getting them to bloom again once the store-bought blossoms faded.

However, I am inspired anew. There is something intoxicating about the prospect of getting flowers from these exotic, mysterious plants.

Like so many successful gardeners, Linda is less than precise in cultivation matters, unable to say exactly when she feeds her orchids ("not very often, because the food is downstairs"), although she swears by the need for humidity and air circulation.

Caressing a mottled-foliage orchid in her living room, she talks about how she and her new plants are in harmony. "They're slow, like I am," she says. "I make it a point to get up and dress every day, but sometimes I've done it at four in the afternoon." The orchid's long-lasting bloom means that "you don't miss it if you sleep all day." She contrasts that with the now-you-see-it, now-you-don't blossoms of the walking iris or the night-blooming cereus.

In the rolling, wooded back yard, inside and outside a little greenhouse, dozens and dozens of plants gather, like refugees from Linda's past, waiting to be replaced with orchids. She says she will try to sell the Indian hawthorn, the hostas, the daylilies.

All require too much care, too much energy. "I don't think I'll get back into the heavy stuff," she says. "I'm resigned to the fact that I'm not the same person."

As fascinating and beautiful as the orchids are, I wondered if Linda would miss the regular old plants, traditional friends that now were leaving to make way for the newcomers.

She acknowledges a "fondness for the plants that have been a part of me" and says she feels a "wistfulness" about losing them but adds that she finds the orchids "satisfying."

Moreover, she says, her slowed pace has made her "more tolerant of older people and their situations." Too, she now takes time to enjoy more of life's natural pleasures, such as birds singing and playing outside her windows.

Sighing, Linda likens her illness and its gardening influences to other life changes. "People have different forks in their roads," she says, recalling the Robert Frost poem, "and they take different paths."

Orchids are hers.

December 9, 1994

SHE LISTENS TO TREES

Rabun County, Georgia — The day was made for walking. Spring warm, with sharp blue skies and huge cumulus clouds floating over the mountains. To the woods we went, Marie Mellinger and I, to see what had risen with the warm weather.

Mellinger is a naturalist, a woman who can walk the woods

and see what most people never would notice. Moreover, she can identify it, tell you what its botanical name is, whether you can eat it safely and, on top of that, appreciate its beauty and historical significance.

On this day, Mellinger and I drive the short distance from her home to Warwoman Dell in the Chattahoochee National Forest recreation area. Visiting this quiet, peaceful place, which was sacred to the Cherokees, in every season for years, Mellinger has identified at least five hundred plant species.

Planting her long walking stick, she moves expertly through the dell, only occasionally making an unsure step that calls attention to her eighty years on earth. She cannot remember a time when she was not actively seeking a connection with nature.

"All my life, I've been crazy about trees," she says matter-of-factly, her voice fading as she darts here and there, bending and peering at something peeping from decayed leaves.

The Crivitz, Wisconsin, native has been loving trees — and everything else that grows from the ground — here in Rabun County for about twenty years. The author of several books on the outdoors, Mellinger conducts seminars on nature, encouraging participants to hug trees. She belongs to a group called the Incredible Edibles, feasting on many plants found in the woods — from poke sallet to sumac brew.

She sells and gives away seeds collected on her walks, hoping to save and propagate native plants. She has packaged her seeds, some six hundred types, neatly labeling them in little envelopes with botanical names and the colorful common ones: goldenrod, pokeberry, yellow-eyed grass, brown-eyed Susan, sourwood, aster.

Mellinger, who reverently quotes Thoreau and dotes on the famous walker's "The Maine Woods," also enjoys mystery novels and Strauss waltzes.

She's busy. But never too busy to share her passion for nature.

Mellinger counsels Rabun County newcomers and longtimers alike, advising homeowners of what grows naturally on their property and how to keep species growing. If her philosophy could be summed up in one of her many sentences on nature, it'd be, "Leave it alone."

On the day we took our walk, you never would have known Mellinger was interrupting a bookful of projects. When we got to the woods, she was as mellow as the day, her enthusiasm for what we found as fresh as the season.

"Oh, look. Look at the partridgeberry!" she said, lithely bending to caress the little evergreen ground cover's showy scarlet berries. While difficult to establish in gardens, the shade-loving plant is sometimes used in terrariums.

She broke a leaf from a little plant she called bulbous cress and handed it to me, saying it tasted like watercress. It did. The yellow violets were "coming out nicely," Mellinger said with excitement. Indeed, the little blooms seemed as much a signal of the season as daffodils in a city garden.

We were never without sound from streams flowing through the dell. But when we reached a clearing surrounded by tall hemlocks, it seemed the quietest place on earth. The hemlocks were sacred trees to the Cherokees, Mellinger tells me. I understood why as we sat on a stone bench, covered with mosses, sunlight streaming into the clearing — through the hemlocks.

There were many more plants to sight, many of which I would not have known. Ferns, orchids that were inconspicuous until Mellinger made over them. Then they grew large. There was spicebush, whose branches were used to make tea. Poison ivy the size of large ropes, climbing to the tops of tall trees.

We tasted birch, which Mellinger remembered as the onetime source for wintergreen. "If you're in a survival situation," she said, "there's enough sugar in the birch — you won't get fat, but you'll survive."

I got a small taste of what it feels like to know things in the woods. We were walking along, when suddenly I saw the familiar forest-green bark of a little understory plant that I grow in a pot. Its strawberry-like fruit cracks open in fall.

"Whoa!" I said. "I know that one. Strawberry bush! Also called hearts-a-bustin."

"That's right," said Mellinger, calmly. "Euonymous amcricana."

Before we parted, Mellinger talked long and passionately about the importance of getting out of doors. "You have to actually tour it and experience it," she said. "All the talking about it and all the seeing it on TV is not the same as feeling it and experiencing it and being out there. It's just not the same at all." (Unfortunately, too many people don't know how to act, once they get out there, littering and carving their initials and names into anything that doesn't move. Tables and benches at Warwoman Dell are no exception.)

Also, Mellinger repeated the message she gives to everyone who'll listen: "Use native plants as much as possible. That helps preserve the species. They're better in drought and better adapted to our soil and conditions than nonnatives. People like to have lawns, but they're a waste of time and effort. Have a wildflower meadow instead of a lawn."

And she told me how she defines a naturalist. A hint: You don't learn it in courses. Mellinger has studied botany and horticulture but not to get degrees. Or to get natural.

A naturalist, she says, is "someone whose main thrust is the out of doors, who teaches it, writes about it, loves it, feels it. I don't think you could be a good naturalist unless you feel it."

She's a good naturalist.

March 24, 1995

FLOWERS OF IRON

Charleston, South Carolina — Philip Simmons, a proud and simple man who turns hunks of iron into intricately beautiful objects, draws inspiration from sources that seem a striking contrast to his beloved heavy metal: flowers and leaves.

These delicate creations of nature, growing all around him at his modest home and shop on Charleston's east side, have been muse and model for the more than two hundred ironworks — gates, fences, window grilles and other useful objects of delight — that grace gardens, homes and churches around this elegant old coastal city.

On the morning after Thanksgiving, when whiffs of oleander and Japanese plum blossoms hung lightly in the heavy sea air, Simmons showed Lyn and me around his place, reflecting on his many years of ornamental ironwork. That work began in the 1930s, as automobiles displaced horse-drawn vehicles and Charleston's preservation movement took hold, transforming Simmons from blacksmith to artist. He now is known nationally and revered here.

In a small room in the front of his home, walls are covered with awards, pictures and certificates paying respect to Simmons' work. Honors include those from the Smithsonian Institution, South Carolina's Legislature and the city of Charleston. There are pictures, too, showing Simmons' strong face and warm, knowing smile.

Among the many official-looking documents is a small poster that reads: "If you want your prayers answered, get off your knees and hustle." Simmons has been doing that since he began shoeing horses at thirteen, apprenticed to a blacksmith who was a former slave.

Now eighty-three and with diabetes and heart problems, Simmons has slowed down a bit, but he still visits schools, demonstrating to youngsters that a black person who is talented and willing to work hard can succeed. Warding off sympathy, Simmons noted, "All my friends passed on with perfect health."

Along with his work and talent, Simmons credits his success to . . . petals, buds, vines and leaves. These plant parts show up repeatedly in his work.

At one point he produced an iron rod about a foot long. Each end had been forged into the shape of a leaf, complete with veins. Then, pointing at a pecan tree in his back yard, he said, "You see those leaves, there? They gave me the idea for this." Simmons uses the rod as a teaching tool, but longer ones could hang curtains.

Magnolias have provided ideas. And palmettos have influenced many pieces — right down to the ridges on the trunks.

At the front of the house are many plants, including jade, aloe, hibiscus, canna lily. The Japanese plum, or loquat, about ten feet tall, grows right next to the porch. All, along with Charleston's palmettos, have provided inspiration during the thirty years Simmons has lived and gardened on Blake Street.

Now, he inspires relatives and other apprentices, including some whites.

On the day we visited, a nephew, Carlton Simmons, started a fire (with the help of some dried pecan leaves) and deftly heated an iron rod, hammering and twisting it into a spiraling, foot-tall letter J. The top is a leaf, a pecan leaf.

As Carlton worked, his uncle, physically unsteady but self-assured, showed us ancient tools, some of which he had made, occasionally opining to Carlton on whether the fire was hot enough and how to shape the piece.

When the iron was wrought, Carlton presented it, telling me, "You can use this to hang one of your flowerpots."

Carlton, now thirty-six, has worked iron since he was thirteen years old. "After a while, it just comes natural," he said.

Does he draw inspiration from flowers and trees, as his uncle has?

"Whatever he does, that's what I do," Carlton said.

It was a proud smile that strolled across Philip Simmons's face. Man of iron. Soul of flower.

December 1, 1995

COACHING A GARDEN

Athens, Georgia — About three years ago, Vince Dooley's gardening curiosity, long overshadowed by his demanding duties at the University of Georgia, burst into daylight. What were the trees and shrubs and flowers growing around his home? Why did they thrive? Where in this rolling, stream-fed landscape would new plants be happy? When should they be planted?

"I'd always been curious, but I'd never had time to satisfy the curiosity," Dooley said as he and his wife, Barbara, led a group of visitors around his garden on a recent muggy, after-rain afternoon. "Now that I've given up coaching, I've been able to do some things that I've always wanted to do." (He was head football coach from 1964 to 1988 and has been athletic director since 1979. To many around here, his first name always will be "Coach.")

With the dedication and zeal that got him inducted into the National College Football Hall of Fame, Dooley set out to satisfy his curiosity, assembling a team of gardening gurus, including UGA horticulture professors Mike Dirr (woody plants) and Allan Armitage (perennials), whose classes he attended on a not-for-credit basis. "I enjoy people who are enthused about what they're doing," he says of the two high-energy, deep-knowledge plant men. Dooley began visiting gardens, collecting plants, devouring knowledge like a hungry man in a room full of food.

"Gardening is my golf," he says.

But before he could truly get into the game, he needed to know what he already had to play with.

So, about two years ago, Dooley telephoned landscape designer Ron Deal, who is co-owner of Classic City Gardens. "We walked around to every plant on the place," Deal recalls, "and I had to tell him the common names and the botanical names. And spell them for him."

Now, Dooley tosses around polysyllabic monikers with the greatest of ease. "He's picked it up quick," Dirr says of Dooley's horticultural learning, "and he's about ready to teach." Dirr seems only half-joking, and Dooley chuckles noncommittally. Too, he plays down the honor many plant people would shout about: He's had a hydrangea named for him, the big blue mophead that stands tall on the side of the house — the one that bloomed last year when most others couldn't get up after being knocked down by the late freeze. On a recent day, blooms from Hydrangea macrophylla 'Dooley' were showed off in a vase in the Dooley home.

The hydrangea is "beyond belief" in cold hardiness, Dirr says. Intrigued by that outstanding property, he propagated the plant and named it for its grower, thus adding another hydrangea to the list of those known. Spreading the word of the discovery, Dirr, a fertile author of reference books on trees and shrubs, has listed the 'Dooley' in his new *Photo-Library of Woody Landscape Plants* on CD-ROM.

Meanwhile, what started off as curiosity has bloomed mightily. Says Armitage, "When he's out here, he exudes joy. He's reached the point he no longer is a dabbler; he's full body in it. He loves it, and he loves sharing it — as we all do — and talking about it."

On the garden tour, Dooley shows off a dazzling collection of trees, shrubs, perennials, a pond landscaped with water plants. His short gardening career already has grown a rich store of stories involving plant swaps, transplanted trees, unusual finds — and of course his early discoveries.

"When I was digging back here — it was a jungle — all of a sudden I stumbled on this," he said, his voice ringing with pride as he pointed toward a magnificent crape myrtle, about thirty-five feet tall, lit by the low western sun. "It was in terrible shape, but we've pruned it, and it's starting to come back. It has a beautiful purple bloom."

Confidently, quietly, he guides the tour all around the house, past the Japanese maples, the hosta, gardenia, viburnum, witch hazel, buckeye, ferns, stones, magnolias, horsetail reed, fringe flower, grancy graybeard, ginkgo, a stand of white pines, discussing them as we go, noting behavior, use in the landscape.

At the perennial garden, Dooley proudly shows off the Japanese iris, astilbe, black-eyed Susan. Behind that are abelia, camellia, hydrangea, backed by a drift of lenten rose. You name it, Dooley's either got it or is planning to get it. "Once I get into something, I don't get into it lightly," he says.

Those who know him well agree. Says Barbara, whose gardening is confined to pots, "Every time Vince picks up a different magazine, he decides we've got to have that."

And Barbara's first cousin, Janet Wells, says, "You just see the energy and drive. If he's going to garden, he's going for a touchdown."

To be sure, Dooley is aware of certain parallels between digging in the dirt and grinding opponents into it. Both satisfy, he says, rewarding hard work.

Football, so much a part of his life for so many years, continues making room for the onetime quarterback's new, softer, passion. You know this when you hear him talk about what he gets from gardening: "I feel good. I thoroughly enjoy working, and I thoroughly enjoy seeing what I have after I work. And I thoroughly enjoy just strolling and seeing — every time I go out — something a little different from what I saw the day before. That's fascinating."

July 13, 1997

WHEN TILLING STOPS

Newnan, Georgia — If we live long enough, sooner or later we'll all get to the time when injury or illness makes gardening impossible. Whether permanent or temporary, an affliction that puts you down at home or in the hospital has a way of putting life — and gardening — in perspective.

Being unable to do something can really help you understand both how important that activity is and how unimportant it is — even gardening.

Britt Flowers is a witness. It was almost a year ago that he and I met in a grocery store here in Newnan, struck up a conversation about chinaberry trees and other delights of the soil. Since then, we've had some great meals together, and we've had a whole lot of fine conversations about our common pleasures.

Sixty-eight years old, Britt is as hooked on digging and planting as anyone I know. Loves growing and talking about everything from muscadines to four o'clocks. And his lush crops show that he's as good a doer as he is a talker.

His driveway is lined with tomatoes growing in big plastic buckets; he prefers growing them this way, as he can just fill the containers with rich compost instead of having to hack through and amend the red clay. Out back, more container tomatoes stand tall and full.

Lately, the vines have been unusually full; starting July 21, Britt spent sixteen days in the hospital undergoing and recovering from surgery to improve his lower body circulation. As his stomach was cut open and a tube shaped like an upside-down Y inserted to move blood to his legs, he is still unable to garden at the robust pace to which he has long been accustomed.

During my visit, we sat outside his home, enjoying one of the five perfect days we get each year in this part of Georgia: balmy, slight breeze, blue skies, low humidity. The huge four o'clock bush by the carport was about to burst into fragrance for the evening, and Britt was talking about his gardening life after this latest surgery (last November, he was operated on to fix a heart problem).

Family and friends have helped a lot during his recovery. "I'm not supposed to do any exerting," he says. "I don't do too much but walk around."

Does this bother him?

"I don't worry about a thing. I take it day by day. This is one of those times in life when it's time to sit back and enjoy what you've already done." What he'd done before entering the hospital was make sure the tomatoes, peppers, onions he'd planted were in good shape, that his old pears, plums and muscadines would produce again this year.

Did he think about his garden while in the hospital?

"I wasn't thinking about nothing. I was in such pain."

So, the garden couldn't hold a candle to his concern for his health. At first. "If you start feeling better, get an appetite, you start thinking about it," he says of his cherished growing space — where he's even planted a little patch of cotton as a living reminder of the crop's historical significance.

Clearly, he was feeling better, plucking tomatoes, filling a basket for me. And, "Look at these muscadines; they're turning. Soon be sweet."

Later, feisty: "As long as I can move, I'm going to do something outside. I'm not going to sit around watching TV. I can't just sit around."

Instead, he's "piddling" around on legs that no longer hurt after ten paces because now they're getting a healthy supply of blood. Usually, he feels real good, but sometimes he feels pain.

He knows he's not supposed to piddle too much. We both know he's racing time, trying to get well before he feels a need to fling himself into garden work.

I can only imagine how tough it is to run that race — to acknowledge that sometimes passions cannot be indulged. Not even gardening.

August 30, 1997

GROWING WORDS

St. Simons Island, Georgia — At last, I have seen Tina's paradise.

For years, my friend Tina McElroy Ansa and I had talked about our writing and our gardening, recounting successes and failures and all manner of joys, disappointments and strangenesses that come with digging in the dirt and coaxing words onto computer screens.

We'd traded stories but never visits. Well, I got to her garden before she got to mine, spending part of a day with the award-winning novelist and her husband Jonée Ansa as he took a break from his latest filmaking project and she took time out from work on her fourth novel (she also is a regular essayist for CBS News "Sunday Morning" and a former writer for the *Atlanta Constitution*).

Now I understand what she's been talking about. On this warm, fat day filled with blue sky, ginger lily sweetness and coastal pungence, Tina's garden wraps its natural, timeless beauty around us and, on a gentle sea breeze, transports us to places of the heart. This garden is a sanctuary on an island that is itself a refuge for many. It is Tina's paradise within paradise.

"I love my yard. I revel in this space, as I do in my Southernness," she says. "When I say 'outdoors,' I mean in my yard, not on a hiking trail or along a mountain stream."

This space, close by the marshes, is not manicured by any means. Naturalists, Tina and Jonee let their plants grow free, if not wild. They prune little. Says Tina, "We're the encroachers. It would be controlling nature to hack through plants. When you have to push through ginger lily, you have to make it a part of you."

This holistic attitude explains why Tina the gardener is inseparable from Tina the writer. The two passions are "intertwined," she says. "My writing and gardening become one. I don't know where one ends and the other begins."

Good. She has made moot the question I can never answer for myself: Which do you love more — gardening or writing?

That done, we tour. "I'm a big believer in fragrance and color," Tina says as we walk among waves and waves of ginger lily, past the soon-to-bloom tea olive, the sadly sweet gardenia, cheerful canna lily and crape myrtle. Past the spot she calls her "comeback place" for the died-back potted perennials, past the collards, orchids, eggplant, rose, tomatoes, Confederate jasmine, the honeysuckle. "I believe in lushness, too, but I get that just from being on St. Simons Island."

To be sure, St. Simons breathes richness. This is a place that makes you believe you could toss a seed onto the ground tonight and awake to a full-grown tree tomorrow. The island's fedundity must help explain its attractiveness to writers — who rarely seem drawn to places like Iceland in search of the Muse.

Tina moved here in 1984, five years before her first novel, *Baby of the Family*, was published (she's now working on the screenplay). Since then, she has written two more, *Ugly Ways* and *The Hand I Fan With*. Her fourth novel, about the decline in care and nurturing of children, is scheduled for publication next year. A native of Macon, Tina sets all her books in the mythical Middle Georgia town of Mulberry.

She recalls how her father once showed her a fountain in Macon, saying it was located in the exact center of Georgia. That image stuck and expanded, making her feel "truly at the center of things."

Now, her center has moved east. In her books' acknowledgments, Tina always thanks St. Simons Island for offering her "acceptance of home."

And a garden that centers.

In her office, the computer sits between two windows, ginger lily growing right up to them. Open a window and the scent jumps inside. Beyond, a cardinal flits through the air. This is what Tina was seeing, feeling, years ago when she and I, in a telephone chat, agreed that the beauty of a garden is so seductive that a writer (or any other worker) sometimes cannot help going to it — no matter what deadline calls.

But beauty is not the whole of gardening for Tina, of course, any more than for the rest of us. While the many garden seats — benches, Adirondacks — invite lolling, strolling, thinking, they also mean, "You can see what needs to be done."

And, especially in this hothouse environment, "There's always something to do. When you come into the garden, you're not doing busy work; you're working." Composting, watering, digging, amending soil, picking off bugs (keep lots of bird feeders to help help control insects, she advises), making insecticidal spray (she mixes a few drops each of liquid soap and mineral oil in a gallon of water).

On this day, there will be no work, however; we are enjoying. Jonee, who sometimes brings home plants to Tina, is pointing out the willows that he bought years ago — he loved them "because they dance." Our cameras drawn, we are shooting happy snaps of one another.

And, befitting good island life, we are sipping Coronas, with slices of a lime that grew on the tree above us. The computers and the fax machines and all other instruments of labor must wait; we're living big in Tina's paradise.

September 6, 1997

Acer japonicum

PART FOUR

TREES

In all shapes, sizes, colors
they lend grace, inspire awe

~

SMALL WONDERS

WHAT I SAW, HEARD and smelled as I gazed lazily out onto my back garden was almost enough to make me believe spring is the loveliest season: flowering almond, spirea, forsythia, all showing off big time; Carolina jessamine in full, fragrant bloom, full of buzzing bees, two blue jays and a brilliant yellow butterfly; ferns returning from underground, along with peony, society garlic, mint and much else.

All of these (and the unfairly maligned photinia, which makes a great specimen plant — just don't plant millions of them) are lovely markers of the season.

But some of my most charming and significant spring companions are Japanese maples, of which I have collected some two dozen in about a half-dozen flavors, including those with finely cut burgundy leaves, some with upright branches, others weeping, some with coral bark or tricolor leaves.

Part of my attraction to these maples is their slow growth, as my garden space over the years has run from miniscule to tiny to small. These trees fit.

Japanese maples herald spring in a powerfully sensual way. And they recall stages of my garden-building, going back almost ten years.

It was then that I bought my first maple — from a nursery in Arlington, Virginia, after falling in love with its delicate, thread-like, burgundy leaves and graceful, weeping form.

The bargain I got on my second maple proved that a good deal might jump into your shopping basket anytime, anyplace. In this case, at a hardware store in Washington. While this tree was about the same size as my first, it cost a fourth as much. I didn't ask why. Maybe it was a bad ad.

We moved the two, along with an assortment of other packed plants, in pots to Atlanta from Washington five years ago. Since then, I have found maples everyplace imaginable — from the *Farmers and Consumers Market Bulletin* to lonely nurseries I lucked up on during automobile trips. One day I found a six-foot specimen sprawled on my walk, unpotted, its rootball resting next to a pine. Sharon Adams, a generous gardening neighbor, had donated it, as she wanted its pot for something else.

Like any loved ones, the maples grow more comfortable each year, settling into their spaces. They are as diverse in their habits as are people; of the two that came from Washington, one has grown horizontally, the other vertically, each about two feet.

And every year about this time, I watch their bones fill out, beginning with little buds that swell and burst with caterpillar-fuzzy leaves.

This early stage invites a caress, in much the same way as lamb's-ears and silver mound, a reminder that plants should be touched as well as seen and sniffed.

As the leaves open, with extraordinary fragility, they assume their shapes and sizes as butterflies do, eventually taking wing on the limbs. Meanwhile, the trees produce tiny clusters of flowers and winged fruit that you can plant. Growing Japanese maples from seed should be left to the long of patience. I finally gained enough to plant seeds last year. I'm still waiting, patiently, for the seedlings, envisioning them as bonsai material one of these years.

It is easy to see and feel why Japanese maples are much of what makes this time so prime. Almost prime enough to displace autumn as the No. 1 gardening season. Almost.

April 1, 1994

HOPES SPROUT BIG

Maybe one of the reasons so many gardeners feel young and keep fresh outlooks is the knowledge that, no matter how long you garden, you're always subject to doing something new.

Well, I'm doing my latest new thing now: growing a sequoia, a redwood. At least, I hope I'm growing one.

What I have is a hunk of reddish wood about the size of a frog; in fact, it looks like a frog. It's a burl, a knot sliced off the trunk of a mother redwood.

Janet Wells presented my burl to me at the end of September, having bought it while she and her husband, Tom, vacationed among the giant trees north of San Francisco during July and August.

Artistic friends who both combine an eccentric sense of humor with deep spirituality, Janet and Tom must have had fun contemplating my reaction to learning that I was getting a redwood for my small garden. At the same time, they knew I would be possessed by the prospect of actually growing one of these awesome trees.

"I've got a present for you," Janet said on the telephone soon after they got back to Atlanta. "It's from California."

"Is it a redwood?" I asked, kidding.

"How'd you guess?" Janet said, laughing. We talked about the redwood for weeks before we arranged for a ceremonial handoff. At one point, Janet had me thinking I was going to pick up a tree at least six feet tall.

I'm glad it wasn't. This burl is much more enjoyable.

When I went to pick it up, it was in what Janet calls her guacamole bowl, which mirrors the brownish-green colors of that wonderfully fattening Mexican delight.

Following directions that came with the burl (bought at a gift shop, dry, wrapped in plastic), Janet had placed the burl in the bowl and added about half an inch of water — like starting a pineapple plant after slicing off the top of the fruit.

By the time I saw it, little green shoots had begun sticking up all around the burl's bark top. Dozens of them. A burl Janet brought back for herself was in its own dish, next to mine.

Like Rorschach inkblots, the pieces of wood invite beholders to interpret their shapes. While mine reminds me of a frog, Janet says hers looks "sort of like a small buffalo." I could see that. A little buffalo whose back sprouts greenery.

Each day with my burl brings something new. Still in the guac bowl, on a table, it is dappled in the parlor's medium light, its sprouts slowly rising, presumably to become trees with scalelike leaves similar to those on hemlocks. Its earthy, piney, slightly spicy smell is a bonsai for the nose, recalling deep woods on rainy days, just as bonsai create forests in miniature.

Never having seen a sequoia but always having loved the idea that the tree was named for a Cherokee chief who developed an

Indian alphabet, I have many questions about this little piece of sprouting red wood (hence the tree's other name). Is it possible to defy geography and grow this tree here? (I know people who say they have grown redwoods outside California.) Will this burl produce roots? Or is it merely a curiosity?

I will consult no experts; I only want time to tell me the answers.

That way, I can look at this chunk of redwood and see the makings of one of California's mature conifers, some 370 feet tall. I see the beginnings of a trunk that will reach an eighty-foot circumference. If I use some of my tree's wood, it won't rot, and it won't burn.

Perhaps anticipating my tree dreams, Tom asked Janet, "Is Lee going to wait for two thousand years to see how that tree develops?" No, holding a redwood in my hand is a pleasure that not even two thousand years can enhance.

October 6, 1995

THE SKELETON LIVES

Believing there should be a peach tree in every Georgia garden, I planted one in a pot last year, a fine young thing, a dwarf that bloomed red and presented me with little peaches that went down with excellent taste.

Well, my peach didn't come back this year, but I have it still. Its skeleton remains in the pot, limbs akimbo. It is more a dwarf than before because, in a futile effort to save it, I pruned it back and back and back until I whittled it down to only about half its former four-foot height.

Nevertheless, the tree is functioning quite well as a resting place for a purple-blooming, variegated-leaf vine I had put in its pot back in the spring — when I thought the peach might survive. I've never known the name of the gift vine, but it couldn't have a better support than the peach skeleton.

I have known gardeners who leave tree skeletons in their spaces as supports for vines such as Carolina jessamine, morning glory and even that tree-size climber, wisteria. Likewise, nature does not always knock down a spent tree before vines claim it for their home.

In both these cases, gardeners and nature know that their trees may be dead in the traditional sense, physically gone, but in another sense they are very much alive, with purpose and value. It is a kind of spiritual recycling. The once-green and growing trees transform into another — leafless — state. One in which they are no longer the stars but play, literally, supporting roles.

On a recent trip to southwest Virginia, I stayed overnight in Roanoke, rising early and heading for the Blue Ridge Parkway. Driving south in the chilly, misty morning, I felt as if I were floating through an other world of gold and burgundy leaves — a world that included huge skeletons covered with fleshy leaves and vines.

The Virginia scene recalled countless ones throughout the Deep South, where often the leaves and vines belong to kudzu. So beautiful, so dangerous, the vines strangle the light from trees until life goes, too — a plant variation on a theme as old as the world: Death wears a lovely mask.

Back home in my garden, I can see close-up how the masquerade works. From the arbor on which it grows, Carolina jessamine repeatedly has made runs at the nearby saucer magnolia, trying to climb all over it. Each year, I beat the vine back, pruning it in late autumn when the tree drops its leaves to reveal how far the jessamine has gone.

Every year, the distance increases. Now, the jessamine almost reaches the treetop, some twenty feet from the ground. I know that, left on its own, the vine would cover, smother the tree, and the scene would be beautiful as the fragrant yellow jessamine blossoms dotted the magnolia. Maybe they would even bloom simultaneously before the end.

I'm resisting that beautiful seduction. As the magnolia leaves drift down, I'm sharpening my pruning shears, readying my ladder.

Having visualized the beauty, I admit ambivalence. A few vines shooting to the top of the tree couldn't hurt it. The prospect of yellow jessamine trumpets amid pink and white magnolia blossoms just may be too charming to resist. Part of me wants to take a chance. The rest of me knows about that slippery slope leading to a skeleton tree: Moderation is not in my nature.

Fortunately, my peach-tree skeleton and its vine bring no ambivalence, pose no dilemmas. Each gives the other a reason for being. That's as close to a perfect relationship as you're likely to find.

October 27, 1995

BEAUTY TO FLAUNT

It was a perfect day for ginkgo-watching: gray and rainy, so the tree's chartreuse-gold leaves shimmered and glimmered seductively, standing out even more than they might in bright sunlight.

The four of us stood admiring the tree, marveling at its perfect color, knowing that its autumn magic was fleeting, half expecting all the leaves to fall in a heap even as we watched. They did not. Even the hard rain could not hurry them off this November day.

Patricia Worrall, who teaches writing at Georgia Tech's School of Literature, Communication and Culture, had organized this ginkgo expedition, which included two of her colleagues, Lissa Holloway-Attaway and Richard Grusin, and me. Taking in the ginkgo's autumn show, we four were joining many other gardeners and tree lovers who find it irresistible.

Part of the tree's attractiveness is its ancient connection. Also known as maidenhair tree because its leaves resemble the fern, the ginkgo is a living fossil, the only survivor in a family that flourished in prehistoric times.

Airy and pyramidal, the ginkgo looks like a mass of butterflies before its leaves drop (all fall in about a week). Close up, the butterflies feel rubbery and are slightly ridged.

Georgia Tech's ginkgo, about forty feet tall, takes on special significance, as it provides a natural counterpoint to Tech's technical bent and to the doggedly utilitarian architecture of the William Vernon Skiles Building that surrounds the tree.

"She's beautiful," said Worrall. "She's vampish." She's everything the building is not.

"She's a survivor," said Holloway-Attaway, whose observation could refer to not only the tree's prehistoric roots but also to her thriving in the academic-industrial complex.

From a balcony, we listened to the rain and watched the ginkgo yellow, counting her attributes and discussing her lore. All agreed on the tree's beauty, and who can deny that a ginkgo styles and flirts with an attitude that says, "I'm sexy." And, yes, this one's very womanish.

There was once talk of naming the ginkgo, but the idea was quickly rejected. How could any name do her justice?

Besides, it makes more sense to practice the Native American belief that an object should be named by each person who sees it a based on what the object means to the individual.

Jo Ann Yeager Adkins, a tree lover and managing editor of the

Chattahoochee Review at DeKalb College, notes that there are at least two ways to spell gingko correctly. She has written a poem, "The Silver Apricot," calling the yellow of the ginkgo leaves a hue to make the brightest sun seem dim.

When the leaves fall, she says:

> I walk between the trees
> Bend to gather all I can of dreams
> I catch and hold one perfect leaf
> To dip in purest gold
> I wear it on a chain about my neck
> It gives me strength to hold a sign,
> Proof that life prevails."

Memories prevail, too. After the leaves have gone, like a lover.

December 8, 1995

SPIRIT BURNING BRIGHT

When I was growing up Down South in Meridian, Mississippi, and Up South in East St. Louis, Illinois, the holiday season wasn't official until we played Charles Brown, singing "Merry Christmas Baby."

In an earthy but courtly manner, Dad would pull Mother into the living room, and they'd slow dance, or slow drag, as we used to call it.

Mother and Dad are gone now, but the tradition continues. These days, Lyn and I slow-drag in the kitchen, one of the few times of the year that I try to dance. Well, there are those Saturday night crab leg orgies, when we put on golden oldies and twist and dip around the room.

But at Christmas time, there's no music like this music. Listen:
Ummmm. Merry Christmas, baby. You sure did treat me nice.
Ummmm. Merry Christmas, baby. You sure did treat me nice.
Gave me a diamond ring for Christmas. Now I'm living in
  Paradise.
Good time Charles Brown. Sing it, Charles.
Here comes my favorite line:
Merry Christmas, pretty baby. You sure been good to me.
Well, I haven't had a drink this morning.
But I'm all lit up like a Christmas tree. Ummmm.

I was so inspired by that line and caught up in the spirit of the season, that I set out the other day to create a giant Christmas tree. Elegant, with white lights.

Believing that an existing tree works much better than buying one and watching it dry out, I have, over the years, strung lights on everything from a Norfolk Island pine to a fiddleleaf fig. One year, I put lights and decorations and such on a pothos climbing up a six-foot slab in a pot.

This year would be different. I decided to move my show out-doors. The Christmas tree would be the saucer magnolia out back. It's about twenty feet tall, and as it is now leafless, I figured it would be a perfect tree, easy to string.

I figured so wrong.

There I was, out there on a stepladder, trying to toss a string of 105 lights (the box notes that in big type) onto the tree. I was about as good at that as I might be in trying to rope a steer. After an obscenely long time, I managed to get the string strung out — all on one side of the tree.

Ah, but I still had another string. Well, in my haste to remove the 105 lights from their snug slots in the box, I managed to lose a few of them. But I decided to toss them up anyway. I figured a few missing bulbs wouldn't make much difference.

Right, wrong again. Without the bulbs, the second string wouldn't light. But I could fix this problem. Just use the extra bulbs so thoughtfully included in the box. So, I plugged in the extras, then plugged in the cord. After about five seconds, the thing began flashing. Instead of an elegantly strung magnolia, I was creating a disco tree.

Only then did I read the directions (who'd ever think you need directions to string lights? The world is getting too complicated.). Seems I had replaced the missing bulbs with those that make the string flash. Elementary, I suppose, for tree-light experts.

I was beginning to wonder if there's something cosmically wrong with swaddling outdoor trees with lights. Was I being sent a message?

Anyway, after another hour or so of switching bulbs and connecting and disconnecting the strings, pruning branches to make room, climbing up and down the ladder, I managed to stop the flashing and get about a third of the lights burning.

Not a huge payoff, considering the time, I figured. Wrong.

When Lyn came home and saw the little swirl of light in the saucer magnolia, along with a swatch I'd rigged on a corkscrew willow out front, she pronounced it beautiful, calling it "magic-land."

And her face lit up like a Christmas tree. Ummmm.'

December 22, 1995

DOWN MEMORY LANE

Greetings of the season. It's Arbor Day in Georgia. Enjoy a tree today.

It is a fine time to plant — and to recall special tree friends we've kwown over the years and to celebrate new ones.

My newest acquaintance is my oldest.

Angel Oak on Johns Island, not far from downtown Charleston, is thought to be more than fourteen hundred years old. Like the many big old trees, Angel Oak, a live oak, keeps its age a secret. The experts can only guess (live oaks tend toward heart rot, making core samples unusable). The city of Charleston owns and operates the Angel Oak site, including a gift shop. Admission's free.

Evergreen, the live oak's leathery leaves grow blue-green from branches that also cradle resurrection ferns. Crevices in the limbs form little pools of rainwater.

Viewed from afar, the ancient tree, with charcoal-colored bark, short trunk and rounded canopy, seems sculpted. When they are very old, live oaks rest their limbs on the ground. Angel does this, inviting children to scamper aboard, as if it were a pony kneeling.

At sixty-five feet, the tree typifies live oaks. They are striking without being a mile high. They are accessible. Their long strands of Spanish moss add a languid touch to the environment.

So it was on the warm day last November when I saw Angel.

There, too, were Terrie Washington of nearby James Island and several members of her family. In her, the tree inspires not only awe but also comparisons with other living things, often human. We are diminished in the presence of a centuries-old tree.

"I look at it and I see how short man's life is," said Washington.

Trees can humble, yes, but they also help us appreciate the power of nature. Nothing on the planet grows large as a tree; a redwood invites an outpouring of superlatives.

Other trees grow fruits and nuts, feeding the body as well as the soul. Some absorb noise, prevent soil erosion, make houses. They give oxygen and increase property values. And they offer play places for countless children.

Today is the day of trees. Like all holidays, this one will focus us for a while. We will think about how to prevent so many trees from being cut down in the name of progress. And we may figure ways to save those we have in an effort to help Atlanta live up to its nickname, City of Trees.

But after the holiday is over, after Arbor Day celebrations have come and gone in other states, as well, advocacy groups will continue thinking on these things. We all should.

February 16, 1996

BITTERSWEET LESSON

The executioners came, as I knew they eventually would. They wore hard hats, yellow with black straps. And vests, Day-Glo red, striped yellow.

They brought a saw. One man placed it at the jugular of the mimosa. As the powerful machine roared and white flecks of wood spewed, another man pushed the tree until it was cut all the way through. For a moment, the ten-foot tree stood, decapitated, balanced on its short stump.

Then, watching the whole thing through the front parlor window, I saw the once-graceful mimosa fall unceremoniously into the wrought-iron fence. A third hard-hatted man helped lift the fresh-cut body over the fence. They dismembered it, limb by limb, and carried the parts to the curb for pickup. One of their own, a fourth man from Georgia Power, silently loaded and hauled away the pieces.

It was over quickly, efficiently.

What had taken six years to grow a — beautiful, sturdy, shade-giving tree whose powder-puff, honey-tasting blossoms delighted the adult me and recalled the child me — was gone in minutes.

Every dead tree has a story.

For the six years I had known and loved the mimosa, it had been on death row. It was an outlaw, growing right next to the three-foot-square green metal underground electrical wiring box in my front garden, despite the warning a black lettering on a yellow background:

NOTICE. DO NOT PLANT TREES/SHRUBBERY OR PLACE OBSTRUCTIONS WITHIN 10 FEET OF THIS SIDE OF CABINET.

The mimosa was a volunteer. Trees don't read. I didn't tell. But Lyn and I knew the mimosa's days were numbered.

Execution day came after a neighboring family lost electrical power. Proving we're all connected — that when one person has a problem, we all have a problem — the box had to be opened to empower our neighbors.

When the power people arrived, I knew they were just doing their jobs. And they knew they were doing me in. Said one, "I'm not enjoying this one bit."

And, to their credit, none of the executioners disparaged the mimosa as a "trash tree," a term that even my friends have tossed at it, despite its evocative name and graceful, fernlike leaves.

Lyn and I are missing the mimosa. As we toured the garden the other day, enjoying winter-thwarted shrubs' new growth and the delayed show of dogwoods and azaleas, Lyn looked toward the place where the mimosa used to grow and said, "Sometimes I almost expect to see it — waving in the breeze."

Yes, we have phantom feeling; we still sense our mimosa, even though it is not there.

Or is it? The executioners left the roots. As spring goes on, there is a chance, a good chance, that the mimosa will rise again. It happened before, in 1990, the first time I saw the green metal box opened.

This prospect of return sets the stage for necessary choices.

I love the tree, but should I allow it to grow again, knowing its endangerment and my pain at its certain loss? Should I Kervorkian it by hacking or putting some chemical on its stump? If I did that, I could plant another mimosa — in a law-abiding spot. Or I could grow both trees, one old, one new.

I am undecided still. Such choices are more easily confronted in the abstract than when reality grows in your own front yard.

April 20, 1996

LASTING CONNECTIONS

At Spelman College a tree grows in memory of Kathryn Elaine Hoffman, a Commerce Department employee who died in a plane crash that killed Secretary Ron Brown and thirty-four others.

In a world so filled with tragedies, accidental and intentional, planting trees as memorials becomes an increasingly valued ceremony, both cathartic and uplifting, a lasting link to people and times no longer with us.

Nothing makes a statement like a tree; its size, durability, usefulness and simple elegance make it choice for honoring and remembering.

As a token of welcome and friendship and, of course, as a way of replenishing war-torn forests, my Israeli hosts in 1978 planted a tree in my name on a hill near Jerusalem. The older I get, the more valuable that occasion becomes. Perhaps that is a reflection of how aging builds appreciation for constancy. A tree certainly represents constancy — even as it changes with seasons.

On the Spelman campus constancy abounds: Hoffman's deciduous magnolia joins many other trees — soaring oaks, majestic elms that escaped Dutch elm disease, flowering cherries.

Over the years, I have gotten to know many of the trees and shrubs on the grounds of Spelman and other Atlanta University Center institutions; they're in my neighborhood, on a route that I used to walk — before gardening became my chief exercise.

A couple of days after the Hoffman tree planting, Keith Clemmons, Spelman's grounds supervisor, and I strolled the thirty-two-acre campus, enjoying the sparkling warmth and chatting about the plantings around the liberal arts college for black women, founded in 1881.

Along with the wealth of trees, the old — and new — brick buildings sit among expanses of grass and focal points mixing shrubs, perennials and annuals.

Some of the specimens amaze. I stopped in awe at Read Hall, where thirty-foot hollies grow. And at Rockefeller Hall, two stands of sweet bay rise some twelve feet. So surprised was I to see these large bays (several gardeners I know lost theirs last winter), I pinched leaves and smelled them. Yes, they are the seasoning. Whatever makes those bays so hardy makes me want cuttings.

As we walked, Clemmons talked about the pride he feels helping Spelman bloom. "This is a top-notch school, and we want it to look like a top-notch school. Parents come to look, and what they see reflects on me as well as on my crew." He likened the campus to his home, saying he wants them both to be beautiful.

Toward the end of our walk, we stopped at the site of the tree for Hoffman, a Wellesley College graduate who attended Spelman for a year. Her tree is the latest addition to a finely landscaped area near Reynolds Cottage, the home of Spelman's president, Johnnetta Cole. Other plantings at the site include hosta, iris, azalea, columbine, yarrow and astilbe.

Days earlier, loved ones had shed tears here. On this afternoon of blue skies, puffy breezes and fatted clouds, Kathryn Elaine

Hoffman's tree, still showing a half dozen unopened pinkish buds, had settled in. Peaceful, serene. Hopeful.

May 11, 1996

PASSION FOREVER

Like the region it thrives in, the Southern magnolia lives large. It is stately and gregarious. It blooms sweetly, always stands out and evokes feelings and memories like no other tree.

Among us Southerners, few are without a childhood recollection of climbing one of these welcoming evergreens, sitting and standing under its comforting canopy, smelling its lemony blossoms on a June evening heavy with dew and promise.

And, as grownups, we appreciate its definitive statement in the garden, in the yard or standing alone, imposing, in a field of sunshine. Fortunately, this adult appreciation enhances that younger, more carefree behavior; it does not replace it. Fact is, magnolia passion is forever.

It is a tree for every season, never failing to impress, with its huge white blooms in spring and summer, dense foliage, leathery green on top and the color of rust underneath. Those showy white blooms age gracefully, turning cinammon, like antique lace, as one magnolia lover put it. In fall, it fruits, its reddish cones turning brown, showing off bright red seeds.

Many single trees are notable, but for group-magnolia drama, I know of no place like the Monastery of the Holy Spirit in Conyers, Georgia.

Fifty magnolias flank the avenue leading to the monastery,

lighting up the space of two to three blocks like scented sentries.

Father Augustine Moore helped plant the trees forty-five years ago, using a post-hole digger on the back of a tractor to site the four-foot trees, now ten times that height. Recently, we walked among the magnolias, inhaling their sweet-but-not-too-sweet lemonness and talking about their appeal.

Father Gus, as he is known, cited their resistance to disease, their beauty, their blooms, one of which "can perfume a whole room." He said he and his colleagues once mulched the trees, "then we found out they take care of themselves."

Magnolia types are many, including deciduous ones such as big-leaved magnolia, saucer magnolia and star magnolia — all of which feel quite at home in the North. But the Southern magnolia, whose botanical moniker is uncharacteristically poetic (Magnolia grandiflora), lives up to its name; although reported to survive north to Massachusetts — as long as it has great shelter — it is Southern to the bone.

John Robert Smith, mayor of Meridian, Mississippi, where I once played among magnolias, recalls the trees modeling for him when he painted years ago: "Magnolias have always been part of a Southerner's still life."

The special magnolia affinity I got from growing up in the Magnolia State persisted through my years in Illinois, Ohio, New York and the nation's capital. When I got back to the true South in 1989, I had to have one of these trees. My space, however, is too small to do it justice. So I bought one called 'Little Gem' and put it in a tub, as the Brits say, where it is fine and dwarfy.

My 'Little Gem' is just a little representation of the real big thing; when I want to see serious magnolias, I go places. Like the monastery. And Tifton. There, a tree called simply the Big Magnolia, estimated to be as old as five hundred years, grows majestically, branches curving to the ground and sending up new trees like a mother giving birth. Close to home, in West End's Howell Park, a group stands, lending year-round beauty to the recently renovated space.

Magnolias, like the region, comfort. Father Gus describes his response on each return to the monastery: "They're really soothing. When I hit this avenue, something happens."

Something happens a lot around the South. Magnolias are common, but never ordinary. And, yes, they're trashy, dropping leathery leaves the way strivers drop names. But trashy isn't necessarily bad.

Mississippians have planted many along I-20, just outside Meridian, livening up that dreary stretch of highway.

And Marcia Bansley of Trees Atlanta says, "We've planted a ton of 'em" since 1992, from four hundred to six hundred. She likens them to iced tea and shade in their evocation of the region's style.

Yes, give them your tired, your hot, your thirsty. After working hard, and playing harder, rest easy. Sheltered, Southern style.

June 8, 1996

A POWERFUL LEGACY

Ever since Opal the hurricane roared through Atlanta almost two years ago, a lot of us have cast worried eyes at our old tree friends whenever the wind blows a bit. We saw the trees that Opal uprooted and wondered which among those left standing were weakened — and therefore threatening.

Some homeowners aren't taking any chances that another big blow will knock a big oak or pine onto their houses; they're beating nature to the punch, having the trees cut down.

Esther Stokes, a landscape designer, has a graphic sense of

the storm's lingering impact: "Opal generated a lot of fear; it really did create a trend. For many people, keeping the trees was a concern."

When a tree falls, the garden feels it. Like so much of the city, my southwest Atlanta neighborhood, West End, is well-treed — oaks, magnolias, pines, pecans. On my property there stands a huge tulip tree, along with smaller dogwoods, saucer magnolia and others. Too, I benefit from neighbors' trees, including the great pre–Civil War oak next door. Its gracious canopy spreads over my roof and garden.

Earlier this year, during one of our windy rainstorms, a younger, but weaker oak, directly across the street tore out of the ground. It fell my way but was mostly caught by the huge oak, which lost a few limbs in the crash.

Swift and certain change came to my front garden, where there used to be bright shade. Shocked by the infusion of light, shrubs already prone to fainting spells, such as the hydrangea and rhododendron, panted heavily and swooned. Hostas and ferns stood, but burned around the edges. Alas, poor acanthus. It may never come back.

On the good side: The additional light benefits the Japanese black pines, which have wanted more for a while. And the redbud, which flowers freely in shady woods, refused to bloom for me this year. If low light was the excuse, that is gone.

Indoors, the front parlor gets more afternoon light, making the aralias and Boston ferns happier.

Still, I'd rather have the tree. In addition to their other benefits — lowering summer temperatures, blocking winter winds, beautifying property, preventing erosion — big trees represent links to our past. How many times I've looked at pictures of homes in which the passage of time is marked not only by added rooms and altered rooflines but also by the height of the tree out front.

As time passed, Atlanta grew, and as it grew and spread, its trees were cut by the thousands. Is Atlanta still the city of trees?

Jay Lowery, the city's chief forester, says that, while applications for permits to remove trees have increased since Opal, the answer remains yes. Great. Yet, we all know you should never take a good thing for granted.

August 2, 1997

Arbor ~ started vine

Carolina Jessamine

Gelsemium sempervirens

yellow flowers ~

PART FIVE

DOWN THROUGH TIME

Years tell essential truths,
teach lessons lasting forever

~

GROWING BETTER WITH AGE

GROWING OLDER SIMPLY MEANS getting better, the argument goes. For some areas of life, that's debatable, but on one matter experts agree: Aging and gardening go together like sun and roses.

Some of us who've been fortunate enough to live half a century are bigger and softer than we ought to be, and getting up in the morning after getting down the night before is tougher than it used to be.

Yes, years do take a toll here and there, but much of what they steal is a small price to pay, considering what they give.

In my case, time taught me something — or helped me feel something — that serves me well as a gardener. I never could have gardened as passionately when I was twenty-five as I do at fifty-two.

Perhaps patience is the thing. Certainly it is one thing. Ironically, patience increases with age, even as our time shortens. Having seen so many starts without finishes, we older folks like to wait and see a thing jell. And anyone who has ever planted a seed or seedling knows that waiting is an essential attribute of the gardening game.

Striving, a frequent byproduct of youth, breeds impatience. How can you please the boss if you don't rush and run? Fortunately, flitting about, whether from city to city or house to house, is increasingly unattractive as years go by.

As necessary as it is, patience alone does not account for intensified passion or interest in gardening. Conversations with other experienced gardeners show a range of changes that help explain the rise of gardening devotion and activity among older people — including increased leisure time and disposable income, nostalgia and the need for permanence.

Also, there's this plain, simple fact: Gardening just feels good. It is a wonderful way to contemplate life's gifts. And as we age, we savor more, having developed greater appreciation for earthly pleasures as well as for mortality.

This is quite unlike our youthful days, when we knew we'd live forever.

Seeing older gardeners move among their plants is much like watching the familiar fashion in which longtime loved ones communicate.

The comfort level is extraordinary as they touch a shrub, caress a leaf. The easiness of movement — unhurried, caring and sure — reflect years of togetherness. Such relationships abound at the home of Thomas (Woody) Oliver, seventy-one, where he and his wife, Christine, have lived since 1958. Six years ago, he traded in a longtime sales career for what has become a full-time pastime.

"He just loves the earth," Christine Oliver explains.

Out of the earth Oliver grows kitchen crops from cabbage to

ginseng and ornamentals ranging from azalea to phlox. A fern-lined stream, alive with minnows and crawfish, provides a cool feeling that came in handy on a recent steamy day as he showed me around, stopping to discuss various plants from time to time.

The oyster plants he grows really do make a good seafood substitute, he says, adding, "I'd like to see more people grow it around here."

A past president of the Men's Garden Club of Atlanta (1991–92), Oliver spends so much time tending plants that he now wonders how he ever had time to work outside the garden.

Of course, the answer is he didn't devote nearly as much time to gardening as he now does. He didn't have the time. Oliver recalls that, in trotting the globe for decades to sell agricultural chemicals, "I may be in Japan this week, Europe the next."

For him, gardening is an antidote to all that. "I've had all the traveling I wanted," he says, counting more than fifty trips to Japan alone. "I'm very content at home."

Years ago, home was the place where Martha Dennis spent a whole lot of time rearing three children and a little time gardening. At sixty-one, she still works (she's a health service technician), but nothing like before.

Even though she was filled with youthful energy as a young mother, she says, "I had to spend it washing, cooking, babysitting."

These days she can tend her roses, clematis, hosta, her tomatoes, broccoli, collards and what seems like a million other plants at her home in West End without fear of passing out from exhaustion.

"I don't have to rush," she says, adding, "and I have more money to spend" than in younger days.

As we lingered in her front garden recently, Dennis gently lifted a clematis vine, praising its blooms over the years, recounting when it commences spring growth from year to year — recollections much like those languid across-the-fence chats parents have about our children.

Some of us garden intensely at midlife because we have so

much time to make up. Rudell Paulette, eighty, recalls how, when she moved to her home in the Inman Park–Little Five Points area twenty-seven years ago, "There wasn't nothing here." There is now, including huge aucuba, hydrangea, azalea, rhododendron and nandina towering over ferns, hostas and begonias — all in her front yard.

In case you're wondering, yes, there can be a downside to being an older gardener.

Oliver has so much time to grow vegetables that friends "roll up the windows to their cars and won't answer the door when they see me coming" with yet another load of tomatoes.

Oh, the humiliation.

Despite such problems, we aging gardeners dig in and hang in, knowing that growing plants while growing old beats the alternative by a bunch.

June 4, 1993

FISH HEADS AND FOOD DYE

Many gardeners say that in a time of increasingly large and impersonal "gardening centers," when more and more hybrid plants are protected and bulked up by pesticides and superfertilizers, they find comfort and stability in simple methods using natural, safe ingredients.

Actress Jada Pinkett's grandmother, who used fish heads as her fertilizer of choice, could have gone down to the local nursery in Baltimore and bought some fish emulsion, but she didn't.

Instead, said Pinkett during a recent visit to Atlanta, her grandmother fed garden plants eggshells, orange peels, "anything that would decompose, but she especially loved fish heads."

Burying a head (or even a whole fish) may increase one's connection with the growing process. Or maybe gardeners just believe it works well.

In any case, there is something about burying creatures that appeals to a lot of gardeners.

Friends of mine, Frank and Edith Stanley of Marietta, love to recount the advice given Frank's father, who tended an estate garden in England for many years, beginning about 1920.

His father was having a hard time getting grapes to grow, so he called on a gardener from another estate to find out the secret of his success. "Bury a dead horse," was the advice.

"Dad didn't have a dead horse, and they wouldn't kill one," he says. But, "A large black labrador was killed in a hunting accident. Dad was told to dispose of it. He buried it under the grape vine. They bore beautifully from then on."

In northwest Atlanta, Catherine Hart took a more vegetarian tack when she wanted to change the color of her hydrangea blooms.

Sure, she'd heard the accepted formula: acid soil for blue, alkaline for pink; add iron or aluminum sulfate if you want blue flowers, lime if you want pink. But did she lime her soil when she wanted to turn her blues pink?

N-o-o-o-o. She added food coloring. Specifically, she used an old jar of paste food coloring that she'd gotten for a pastry-cooking course back in the '70s.

Why? Because it was there, she says, noting, "I couldn't use it for cooking; it was too old."

It was back in the early '80s that it first came over her to use the food coloring. In spring, she put less than an ounce in the soil around one hydrangea. "At first, the color came up through the leaves," she says. "Then they turned back green the next year or two."

The blooms changed to pink the first year, she says.

Alongside the house, a twenty-foot row of hydrangeas, which

Hart began planting more than twenty years ago, shows a lot of pinks among the blues. "I like them better than when they were all one color," she says, adding that she has put food dye in the soil to turn white hydrangea blooms blue at her son Michael's home in West End.

Several plant experts were surprised or doubtful that food dye would work on hydrangeas, but since they hadn't tried it, none could disprove its effectiveness.

Hart, a retired Fulton County employee, is no scientist, but she deduces of the food coloring, "If it does this (dyes food), then I say it ought to do that (dye flowers)." Her bottom line: "It works."

I've been told about a concoction used to fight worms and bugs on tomatoes and potatoes: chopped elderberry parts (leaves, stems), mixed with tobacco and water. This is way beyond ashes, which a lot of people use for the same purpose.

Such organic approaches resonate with Bobby and Richard Saul, owners of a wholesale nursery that bears their name.

Bobby says they've been using a mixture of a teaspoon of baking soda in a gallon of water to treat plants with powdery mildew. Spraying plants like phlox and verbena has "actually knocked it (the mildew) down," he says.

And Richard recalls a landscape architect who swears by the age-old practice of throwing soapy water on plants to kill insects and liven up the plants. Richard says putting a little mineral oil on corn silk keeps worms off the ears.

Bobby believes there is an increase in such practices, asserting that it is part of a "resurgence in old-timey plants. People are going back to things that are natural, tougher and more environmentally safe."

As enthusiastically as many gardeners embrace pet practices for making plants flourish, sometimes nothing works like a threat.

Frank used it on a fig tree in his front yard eight years ago when the tree started dragging its feet after some productive years.

As Frank's wife, Edith, a newspaper bureau researcher, tells it, "Frank went outside and told this fig tree that if it didn't bear fruit, he was going to chop it down. I guess it listened. Since then, we have had so much fruit that we've had enough to barter."

And to give away, as well. I bear witness.

July 2, 1993

ROOTS AND HOME RMEDIES

Born in the country and raised in a small Southern town, I thought I knew a little something about plants in folk medicine. But after a close look at the Quarry Garden at the Atlanta History Center, I know just how little I knew.

In Cuba, Alabama, my mother's mother used to boil pine needles to make a tea that we drank for colds. Then there was mullein, which I remember as resembling giant lamb's-ears. Its leaves or flowers made tea for coughs. And, like many country boys, I used to chew the hardened sap from sweet gum, in lieu of store-bought gum. I don't know if it was medicinal, but it sure was soothing.

As an adult, I have seen fascinating displays of plant parts in health food stores and in more mysterious places that cater to root doctors, hoodoo folks and conjurers.

But Sue Vrooman, a horticulturist at the history center, showed me things I'd never seen.

She tends the Quarry Garden, an easy, peaceful space with a trickling stream, soaring trees, craggy granite and some three hundred plants — most of them native to Georgia and including many that the Cherokee Indians and other Southerners used as medicine and remedies for myriad problems — from coughs to fleas to difficult childbirth. Several had to do with combating snakes.

Warning: Do not try most of what follows at home, as the percentages of ingredients and their effectiveness are not known. Among the exceptions: using dogwood twigs as toothbrushes — something I'm about to try.

Much of this plant information has passed on with those who held it years ago, leaving us to patent medicines, particularly in urban areas. Some of the plants have passed on, too, except for those kept in gardens like this one.

As we started our stroll on a cool, breezy day — under the sycamores, pines, dogwoods, bald cypress, sweet gum, beech, among the shrubs, above the emerging perennials — we passed a red buckeye tree, which supposedly provided a magic grenade for anglers.

"You take the seed, mash it up . . . throw it into the water and it will stun fish, temporarily," says Vrooman, adding that lore has it that "You can scoop them out."

At the partridgeberry, an evergreen trailing plant that produces red berries, she noted that Indian women used the plant in a tea for several weeks preceding the time for their babies' births. It was supposed to ease and speed delivery.

Because births were "risky times" hundreds of years ago, Vrooman says, people sought assistance through plants, "anything that could strengthen contractions, stop bleeding, induce the flow of milk."

A biologist by training, Vrooman has a special interest in ethnobotany and says each Indian nation had its own way of using plants as remedies, as did every ethnic group that came to the region. For example, she says, Cherokees used the bark, twigs and leaves from the east side of trees because they believed that side was the source of strength. Often, she says, Indians would test remedies on prisoners.

Vrooman and other experts make no claims that all these plants work as historical accounts say they do, noting that attitude and belief play a role in whether a remedy is effective. Often, they say, what one believes is what is.

The uses and nicknames for plants seem limitless. Sedge as a diarrhea antidote; leucothoe, called doghobble because it would entangle dogs as they chased bears; strawberry-bush bark to stop dandruff; rhododendron as camouflage for whiskey stills because it grew along creeks that provided water for 'shiners.

And then there are the snake-remedy plants.

Barren strawberry, a ground cover about six inches high, was smashed and applied to snakebites. Rattlesnake plantain, orchid-like and with variegated leaves, was used in a poultice for the bites. The root of Solomon's seal, a perennial herb with cream-colored flowers, was supposed to repel snakes.

(For many years I have known Solomon's seal as John the Conqueror, a mainstay for root doctors, who say it is all-powerful, able to do everything from fixing your love life to leading you to a winning lottery number.)

While many took an aggressive stance toward snakes, somebody long ago hit upon the idea of trying to befriend them. Thus, Vrooman says, "Certain plants were supposed to draw snakes as protectors." Ginseng was among them.

From snakes to bugs: Bloodroot was used for a dye and for repelling insects. Humans, though, love its beautiful, brief white flower.

Witches, of course, also were a big problem years ago. So, "witch punishers" drank a brew made with wood rush "for strength," says the label on the plant.

Before store shelves were chock-full of cosmetics for every need, many people made their own. Among the fragrant plants used was wax myrtle, whose berries were used in soap and candles. Not surprising. But I was surprised to learn that the plant was once spread around the home to repel fleas. And placed under and over freshly slaughtered beef to keep flies away.

Reflecting a belief among Indians and Europeans that a plant's shape dictated its medicinal use, liverwort, with lobed leaves resembling a human liver, was used for liver complaints and lung afflictions.

In this garden, visitors teach as well as learn. Vrooman recalls one woman who saw a daisylike plant and marveled that it was on display. "We call that 'wet-the-bed,'" the woman said. "Mama told me if you touch that plant, you'd pee in your bed." Turns out the plant is a diuretic.

Especially poignant is the account of how horsemint, with its pungent fragrance, was used in a compound to "rally the dying," the plant's label says.

While one tribe used it to stimulate the heart, another found it useful for relieving backache. If you rub oil from its leaves on your skin, you'll sweat.

It is impossible to walk in this space and not feel something special. As Vrooman puts it, it is like being "in the womb of the Earth."

For me, a visit to the quarry garden is, in some ways, like times I have spent at Civil War battlefields. In this garden, as on those killing grounds, the air is charged with past lives and deaths.

March 18, 1994

HOPE SPRINGS PUNGENT

As I write this, I am sitting in my back garden on Easter Sunday, feeling pleasures rush in on sights and sounds of flowing water, cooing doves, buzzing bees, swaying branches, butterflies and Japanese maples.

It is a day of hope, embodied partly in the little patches of food I planted the day before: seeds for tomatoes, peppers, cilantro and okra. You never know what you're going to get, if anything, when you put seeds in the ground. But just after you plant, you always believe. And you hope.

There is hope, too, and delight in the smells — new roses I just brought back from a little nursery near Meridian, Mississippi, the Scotch broom that shook off its doldrums after I gave it more sun (it promises to stay healthy).

And there's one more smell of hope and delight that is increasingly important: manure.

On this day, it is freshly turned into the earth, watered and warmed by the sun. My composted cow manure is delightfully fragrant, pungently making the point that it is the best way to grow. Some springs I spread only composted leaves. This is a manure year.

Many years ago, I never would have thought it possible to sit down with somebody and have a long, interesting conversation about . . . manure. But I did just that recently with Peter Majaya — and found it inspiring. The older I get, the more I want to protect my little piece of land from chemical harm.

Majaya (pronounced mah-JAH-yah), an anthropology devotee who has a fledgling landscaping business, refuses to use any unnatural chemicals in his planting, fertilizing and pest controlling. When he talks about manure, which he gets from stables, his voice grows excited, and he radiates joy. Majaya is a true believer.

As Suzanne Jonap — she and her husband, John, were Majaya's first clients — puts it: Organic gardening "is almost a religion to him. He does it with lots of love and care."

As it happens, Majaya began gardening organically a couple of years ago when he lived at an Atlanta temple with members of the International Society for Krishna Consciousness, growing food and flowers in exchange for a place to stay.

Benny Tillman, temple president, and his wife, Wanda, remember Majaya as a master at growing incredibly sturdy impatiens, daffodils and other plants. "He did a very nice job," recalls Benny Tillman. His wife says Majaya put "so much love and devotion into gardening. It wasn't ordinary."

Majaya says, "They are so much into natural things, it would have been contradictory of me to ask them to buy fertilizer. They don't even drink coffee or Coca-Cola."

Born in Harare, Zimbabwe, thirty-seven years ago (when it was Salisbury, Rhodesia), Majaya came to America in 1983 and began studying anthropology at the University of Tennessee–Chattanooga. In 1989 he left school and moved to Atlanta, "a magnetic town," where he took a job at a landscaping company, planting shrubs and trees.

By last year, when he began organically landscaping at the Jonap home, planting grass and flowers, including tulips, daffodils and poppies, Majaya's stint at the temple had made him shun man-made chemicals ("Nature provides its own fertilizer"). He dug up the yard, pulling out weeds, aerating and mixing in "truckloads and truckloads" of manure. He calls the Jonaps' lawn "the best-looking grass in the neighborhood."

Credit manure, Majaya says. He's happy to see increasing appreciation for recycling this waste material and acknowledges that many of us compost leaves, grass and other yard waste these days. But he wants to see other recycling as well, recalling life in his home country, where practically nothing went to waste, including paper, bottles and cans. In America, he says, "We tend to forget that nothing is useless."

Instead of spraying commercial bug-killers, Majaya advocates simply growing strong plants, noting that healthy plants are the best pest-fighters known. ("Nature has a way of taking care of itself.") Also, of course, there are myriad natural concoctions, using everything from ashes to garlic to tobacco.

And, experts say, pest populations can be repelled by "ally" plants, those that protect "target" plants. Example: garlic planted near lettuce supposedly controls aphids. Too, you can diminish pest numbers by bringing in their natural enemies and encouraging birds to visit your garden.

He concedes that gardening organically does not necessarily mean you get more beautiful plants than with man-made chemicals. "A tulip is a tulip," he said, laughing deeply. Then, evaporating even the hint of a smile, he adds, "But when you use only what nature provides, you are showing much more environmental and ecological awareness. You are getting back to basics that mankind has used through the ages."

That makes a tulip much more than just a tulip.

April 21, 1995

CAR'S GOOD DIRTY WORK

Like an old house full of good ghosts and delightful memories, my aged automobile has a lot of stories to tell. Many of them are about plants.

Bought new in the suburbs of Washington, D.C., in 1986, the light-blue Honda Prelude immediately was pressed into service as a plant hauler. More practical people bought trucks for this purpose, but not Lyn and me. Not only did Yosh (we name everything from cars to alarm systems around our house) take us on Sunday drives through the beautiful Virginia countryside, he also carried ferns and maples and pines and much more to our home on Capitol Hill.

Since 1989, Yosh (rhymes, ironically, with gauche) has lived in Atlanta — as have Lyn and I — and he has traveled much of the eastern United States, from New Jersey to Louisiana. These trips have varied, ranging from sublimely happy vacation trips to ridiculously tragic news assignments. They all shared one trait: Each was an opportunity to collect a plant or a few. And Yosh always was a willing worker. Many of the plants went into the trunk, of course. But when that was full, the rest went inside. And some of the taller specimens had to go up front, with the seat fully reclined. Man, what a great feature that is for plant addicts.

Over the years, all those drippy pots and soggy soils took a dirty toll, despite my uneven use of paper protection; Yosh's erstwhile medium-blue carpeting looks about like a white dog that has been wallowing in a coal mine for a few years, giving new meaning to the expression ground-in dirt.

Every once in a while, I (his primary driver) treat Yosh to one of those expensive shampoos, where he gets "detailed," much the way the people at the cat clinic clean up and perfume our cats. Well, he smells good for a while, but by now the ground-in dirt has become a permanent carpet component. There are few truly blue fibers left.

That grimy reality recently drove me to make a deal to replace Yosh's carpeting. Never had I considered such a move, although I have driven several cars into the ground. But, then, never had I ever hauled so many plants that the ground was so driven into the carpeting.

Looking over Yosh's insides the other day as the carpet man and I did our deal, I focused on dirt spots that the car displays like gardening trophies and tried to connect them to the plants they represented.

One of the first big ones was made by our first Japanese maple, bought in Arlington, Virginia, in 1988. We were so numbed by the tree's tall price we were oblivious to the smudging it was giving the carpet.

Twenty boxwoods hauled from Charles City, Virginia, to Atlanta in 1992 set the record for distance in our plant-hauling treks. But the native azaleas from Fairhope, Alabama, and the yucca I bought on the way back from South Carolina got a pretty good ride, too.

Several of those spots belong to giant houseplants that I bought one brutally hot day in Snellville, just north of Atlanta, where I had gone to interview people for a story about conflict over the building of a synagogue.

I had a little time to kill before my first appointment that afternoon in 1989, so naturally, I sought out a nursery. In those days I was buying furiously for both indoors and outdoors, as we had only been in our home for about a year. I still don't know how I did it, but I stuffed into the inside of that little two-door car a seven-foot tall pothos whose many vines twirled around a tall slab of wood. Also, I bought a fiddle-leaf fig, about the same height. Not stopping there, I squeezed in a couple of four-foot cacti, several ferns, a couple of gardenias and some soil.

The day was so hot I was afraid that any of the plants would fry if I put them in the trunk, so I put them all in Yosh's cabin. As insurance against the heat, I left the engine — and the air conditioner — running during each of several stops for interviews. Those Snellvillians I talked with must have thought I was in a frightful hurry: "No, I'll leave it running, thank you."

The hauling continued, including several Japanese black pines, maples galore, cherry, magnolias, some balled-and-burlapped, others in pots. Myriad shrubs and perennials all have ridden with the unwaveringly dependable Yosh. All have left traces.

Now, as I prepare to have those signs removed, a little of me does wonder if I am losing something I will miss. Yosh's new carpet will be much like a new house. Pristine, yes. Fresh-smelling and plush-feeling, too.

I am sure I will enjoy sliding my feet through its fuzzy newness, admiring its factory blueness. But Yosh's new floor will have no travel tales. It will be adventureless. It will have no earthly connection to the garden that Yosh helped build. Not for a few days, at least.

June 23, 1995

LOVING AND LEAVING

Every time I've left a garden — and I've left a few — I have mixed feelings about whether I want to see it again.

When I've moved to a new city and visited the old one, part of me wanted to drop in on the old garden to see how it had matured, what had been added, what was in bloom. What had died or been removed. But another part of me didn't want to risk seeing my old space in decay, ignored. Or (and this is unreasonable jealousy, I know) like an old lover, flourishing in the hands of someone new.

I don't know whether some professional designers have similar feelings, but I do know that Takeo Uesugi does not shy away from return visits. The West Covina, California, landscape architect designed Hotel Nikko's Japanese garden, which opened in 1990, and he comes back and back and back, charting the garden's course and consulting with people from the firm that maintains the garden.

"I've come to see my baby," Uesugi said during breakfast the other day. "I do that once a year."

My conversation with him came a few months after I had met

Toshihiro Sahara, the master craftsman whose wooden structures live in the hotel garden. Uesugi's passion for putting plants and stone and water in pleasing arrangements complements Sahara's passion for creating a fine gate or bridge. Taken together, the two conversations give me a good inside look at the building and being of a Japanese garden. While Sahara spoke fervently of the harmony between people and the wood he works and loves, Uesugi focused heavily on the people-to-people contact that he hopes his design inspires.

What does Uesugi think of his garden baby these days?

"It looks fine," except for the damage left by leaf-gnawing pests, he said, noting that, like any garden, this one has improved steadily as it grew toward the magical five-year mark, the time experts say it takes for a space to come together. Azaleas, rhododendrons, ferns, mosses, bamboo and Japanese black pines seem more at home together than five years ago, Uesugi said, noting also that a row of pines designed to screen out the surrounding Buckhead buildings now accomplishes its mission.

During his visits, Uesugi can't keep his hands off the garden. Just before our breakfast, he had been pruning. "I just changed my clothes," he said, chuckling. Later, in the garden, I saw the snippets of pine and azalea lying where they had fallen. Said Uesugi, "I think landscape architects should be doing this — cutting trees and shrubs" because it gives them a better sense of how their creations work.

Calling Atlanta "one of my favorite cities," Uesugi said he views the garden here as a kind of "cultural exchange" that helps Southerners and Japanese people know each other better. (Our Japanese breakfast, too, was doing its part, as it included rice and toasted fish, always a winning combination for this Southerner.) The cultural exchange promises to intensify: Uesugi is planning a five-acre garden in Mobile.

Returning to Atlanta each year constitutes "a learning process for me," said Uesugi, who teaches landscape architecture at California State Polytechnic University in Pomona. "I learn if the plants are working well, how to design next time."

Like so much in Atlanta, the garden carries big hopes of impressing the many visitors who will be drawn to the city for the Olympics next year. The five-year maturity came just in time, it seems.

Lowering his voice for emphasis, Uesugi said, "This garden will be so beautiful next year. This year, I'm going to do something, but I'm looking at next year." He said, for example, that he wants more ground cover for the artificial rocks and will do no severe pruning — just touching up, the way a man resists cutting his hair real short to avoid looking looking too fresh. A natural, harmonious look derived from much attention is a basic characteristic of the Japanese garden.

"I want people to see that this is a Japanese garden," he said, "grown in Atlanta. My idea is that a Japanese garden could be anywhere, just like any other part of culture." He went on to point out that Japanese gardens symbolize serenity. "If people feel that way, I'm very happy to see that," he said.

Walking through the garden, on a remarkably tolerable summer day, Uesugi reveled in the beauty of his baby and talked about what makes him design others and keeps him coming back for visits. "I love being able to work with nature," he said, accompanied by songbirds trilling in the background and with the sight of aggressive mockingbirds hovering to ensure that we didn't get too close to a nest in a nearby pine.

Uesugi said that, as far as he can tell, it is "very seldom" that landscapers return annually to a garden they've built. For him, however, each visit seems a happy homecoming. His pleasure at coming back almost made me amenable to seeing what the new homeowners have done to my garden on Capitol Hill in Washington since I left it in 1989. Maybe I'll check it out this summer. Maybe.

June 30, 1995

Rabbit's foot fern

PART SIX

INSIDE, OUTSIDE

Blending, so we do not notice
where one ends, the other begins

⁓

DEGREES OF SEPARATION

AFTER MOVING TO ATLANTA'S West End in 1989, it didn't take
me long to run out of ground in my gardening spaces, front and
back — even given the inevitable binges of ripping out plants.
They were always replaced quickly with others.

So, when my plots were as full as I could stand and as close to
stable as a garden ever gets, I brought in pots to accommodate
those irresistible newcomers I continue to buy and receive from
friends.

Often, when I visit a nursery, just to look, I hear a plaintive
cry: "Buy me. Buy me."

I succumb, not having a clue where I'll place the insistent little thing. But I've never seen a gardener who hasn't room for one
more plant.

So, with dozens of pots scattered about, I have for years viewed each freezing season with a certain dread, even as I rejoiced in anticipating the break from constant watering and pruning.

Each year about this time would come the potted-plant questions: Which ones need to come inside? How long can they stay outside? And where will they go once I haul them in? (Funny how indoor space gets eaten up as soon as a plant vacates it.)

Winter already has fired warning shots of subfreezing temperatures, reminding me of past rituals. For example, several years ago, while traveling, I heard a weather report predicting a hard freeze for Atlanta. I immediately telephoned home with detailed instructions on which pots to bring in, where to put them, when they might be returned outside.

Well, good-bye to all that.

This year, I'm taking a different tack; those living outdoors must take their chances, no matter how low the thermometer goes or how long it stays there.

Just as seeing children leave home brings more room but a certain emptiness, putting plants on their own for a winter has both pluses and minuses. The pluses are more numerous.

To avoid making this a rashly cruel change, when spring came this year, I did not put as many indoor plants outside as in past years. A favorite orange grown from seed, for example, stayed indoors, despite my fear it might be set upon by whiteflies again. (It wasn't.)

But I did put some out there, including a potted palm, Norfolk Island pine, primrose and some ferns.

Along with these, some traditionally outdoor plants, such as oleander, beg to be taken in for just one night or two during severe cold spells.

Also among those begging to be brought indoors are some tender herbs and a few tropical-looking mystery plants I picked up here and there.

All of these beggers, however, must stay outside. There's no room in the house.

One exception. In October I put out three Christmas cactuses to set buds. I brought them in around the first of November. But that's it. Not even the Venus flytraps get to come in this year.

I have come to appreciate the stability that comes from leaving indoor plants indoors and outdoor plants outdoors. And I'm happy not to lug around the heavy pots.

This decision in some ways makes me feel like part of an ancient culture, one in which elderly or ailing family members are set out on the ice when their earthly visit appears over.

Of course, if some plants prove fit for the cold and survive, I'll welcome them heartily in the spring and salute their hardiness. If they don't make it, I will miss them. But their successors will constitute fresh additions next year.

As in so much of our lives, the two extremes are separated by but a few degrees.

November 12, 1993

LIGHTING MOMENTS

Real estate agents often say the three most important factors in buying a house are location, location and location. For me, the three are direction, direction and direction.

The first thing I look at in choosing a house is the way it sits on a piece of land, the directions the windows face, because that, along with positions of trees, will tell me how much light I'll have inside.

Getting good light (and not shutting it out with drawn

draperies) is akin to buying a good, sturdy kitchen table; both are essential furnishings.

In our 104-year-old house, natural light is especially important because we have dark walls (red, blue), framed by lots of dark wood, and we removed all the ceiling lights, replacing them with fans. So for daytime illumination, it's either the sun or table and floor lamps; candles and oil lamps on stormy days when Georgia Power fails.

To be sure, part of my motivation for wanting a house furnished with good natural light is that it nurtures plants, which also are essential furnishings.

(I even borrow light from a neighbor's white house, using the reflected rays to grow African violets in my north window. Maybe I should ask him to agree never to paint his home a darker color.)

But beyond its importance to plants, the light inside a house plays a unique role, creating scenes and moods that no other furnishing can duplicate.

In our home, whose back faces east, morning lights the kitchen with a chipper glow that makes us more ready than we might otherwise be to face a day regardless of what we did the night before.

No radio, no television can send the same message in the unobtrusive yet insistent way that a set of warm rays does: Hello, it's tomorrow. Wake up and take a look.

As it travels over and around the house, the sun reaches into the dining room soon after noon, lighting the Boston fern on the mantel, then polishing the top of the oak table before glinting off frames around pictures of family members, reminding us of times and people gone by.

"Moments," Lyn and I call these sightings of sunlight playing with other furnishings in our home.

Perhaps our favorite moment is the one in late afternoon when the sun sets across the street and streams in through the stained-glass window in the parlor, simultaneously streaking through a clear-glass sidelight by the front door and throwing its flower-petal pattern onto the hall wall.

This moment, lit better than any electric system could accomplish, speaks with more authority than a handcrafted organ, is more melodious than a concert piano.

Look at this light, and pop the cork on a bottle of champagne. You'll never again miss the sunsets of Santa Barbara and Key West.

In certain places we wouldn't dare consider putting another piece of furniture; those spots are reserved for light.

Just inside the dining room, light lands on the pine floor and belongs there as surely as if it were a table or chest. And on the blue velvet sofa, light adds tone as deftly as any scarf.

Even for light lovers, there comes a clash between desire for openness and need for privacy.

Such was the case with our bathroom window upstairs. Block glass solved the problem, allowing us to shower without entertaining the neighbors.

No such problem elsewhere; shutters and blinds on windows allow both maximum openness and complete closure.

Like other pieces of furniture, light can grow a bit predictable; after a few years, you may begin to see it the way you see an aging sofa: time for a change.

We reached such a point this year. The light on the wall leading upstairs didn't do enough for us anymore. So, a couple of months ago, we found a vertical mirror that just fit the spot, giving us a wonderful new piece of reflected light.

On that wall and all through the house, the three most important pieces of furniture are light, light and light.

January 21, 1994

FENG SHUI

In the small Chinese herb shop he manages on Buford Highway, David Chen is telling me about feng shui, the ancient Chinese art of placement, drawing diagrams and making notes in Chinese on a yellow legal pad.

Pulling out a compass, he takes a reading to show that the shopfront faces southeast. Also, his desk faces the door, and, thankfully, no skyscrapers loom over the front of the low-rise shopping center.

Each of these points, and many more, are important to those who practice and believe in feng shui (pronounced fung shway), which uses placement to put you in harmony with your surroundings. When a feng shui practitioner like Chen walks into a business or home, he will examine the way the structure sits, along with the way furnishings and furniture are arranged, to evaluate its feng shui. Through the ages, practitioners have even consulted on how to place family gravesites.

While I have always insisted that my front door face west because that insures good natural light at various times of day, some feng shui experts might differ, citing my date, hour and place of birth — and other factors.

In any case, good feng shui means good luck, health and wealth, thus many people are willing to rearrange their environment to promote a harmonious flow of cosmic energy, or ch'i.

While feng shui (literally, "wind and water") is familiar to most Chinese people, it is relatively exotic to others. Chen is doing everything he can to change that. He counts close to one hundred members of other ethnic groups among his five hundred clients, most of whom are in the Atlanta area. His fee for a feng shui consultation is $170, he said, and he charges $50 to chart your birthday's meaning in your life.

A slight man who wears wire-rimmed glasses and a shadow of a moustache, Chen, forty-three, used to run a business that produced automobile headlights in his native Taiwan. He closed the business, began studying feng shui and, three years ago, moved to the Atlanta area. He lives in Chamblee with his wife, Sherry, and their three children.

In our talk about feng shui, he explained that by facing southeast, the herb shop is in harmony with his energy. Because his desk faced the door, no one could make a surprise entrance and break up his ch'i. And the absence of a tall building out front ensures that energy can flow freely.

Chen is one in a long line of feng shui practitioners. The art combines Tibetan Buddhism, Chinese Taoism, a lot of common sense and a bit of country lore. Like so much in life that cannot be explained by science alone, feng shui seems to work if you believe it works.

My attitude is, if you walk into a home or business, and something just doesn't feel right, the feng shui is bad. On the other hand, if the space is inviting, making you feel good, the feng shui is good.

Sarah Rossbach lives in the New York City area and has studied under Lin Yun, the legendary authority on feng shui. Rossbach consults and has written several books on the subject. She said that while there are many schools of feng shui, the art essentially deals with "how you emotionally respond to your environment. The aim has always been the same: to enhance the lives of residents."

While feng shui has stood time's test, it also historically has been rife with charlatanism. Many Chinese today view it with a mixture of curiousity, bemusement, respect and skepticism. Virtually no one will say outright that it does not work.

Raymond Hsu and his wife, Anna, consulted a feng shui practitioner for their old restaurant in north Atlanta about five years ago. "It was surrounded by highrises," he said. That's bad feng shui.

The practitioner looked the place over, took readings with his compass and came up with several recommendations, including making an additional back door. "The front door and the original back door were aligned," Hsu said, "so he advised us to open up another door and break up the bad luck. The second entrance cancels out the bad effect, creating a kind of zigzagging."

Alas, that restaurant closed in 1992, and Hsu opened another in downtown Atlanta that same year. "We had a brief review" of the current place, Hsu said, and the feng shui was okay. "Basically, it was the front door, which way it was facing. If a highrise is right in front of you, generally speaking, it's not very good for you. He found the restaurant was not in danger."

The other day, when I learned that the element water is of prime importance to my ch'i, I concluded that that helps explain my love of gardening (water feeds the element wood) and my urge to buy two aquariums.

Does feng shui work?

Just about everyone practicing it has the same answer: Can't hurt. That works for me.

August 5, 1994

PEACEFUL DOWNPOUR

Gutters. What are they good for?

Absolutely nothing.

And that's why I recently relieved our house of them. Utterly gutterless, I've seen no catastrophes so far. Just the opposite. The change has even helped my garden.

Okay, saying gutters are good for nothing is overstating the case — slightly. Gutters and downspouts do allow you to stand on your steps without getting drowned by water running off the porch roof. And if you have a basement, maybe a system of gut-ters will transport the water away from the edge of your home, keeping your belowground quarters out of harm's way.

But having no basement in my century-old house, and not spending a lot of time standing in rain from the porch roof, I had been looking for a gutter justification since moving in six years ago.

Most experts — homeowners, builders, gutter repairmen, roofers — warned me to leave the gutters alone. But nobody had a truly convincing argument for keeping the things. "You'll erode your foundation," "The house'll look strange without them," "They're on there, so they must be necessary" were the best rea-sons I heard.

On the other hand, I had plenty of reasons to take them off. As many reasons as there are leaves and acorns from the pre–Civil War tree next door. And in my own yard is a sixty-foot tulip tree that produces endless numbers of tulip-shaped yellowish flowers in spring and banana-colored leaves in fall. Together, these two specimens alone discard more tree parts than any gutter system could ever handle.

Add the rest of the neighborhood trees, and I was getting enough compost and mulch material to require gutter cleanings a half dozen times a year.

The leaves began backing up, damming the water, which rot-ted the wood behind and under the gutters. Clearly, something had to be done. But before I did it, I checked out other houses, seeing how the gutterless fared.

In Lumpkin County Richard Saul, co-owner with brother Bobby of Saul Nurseries, showed me an example of how the old-timers around the North Georgia mountains planted patches of sedum — they called them houseleeks — around the drip line of houses to catch and divert water as it cascaded off the roof.

During a trip to coastal Georgia last June, I spent part of a day with T. Reed Ferguson, historian, author and ten-year resident of St. Simons Island. As we toured the Hamilton Plantation site, I noticed that, among the sumptuous begonia, gerbera daisy, periwinkle, daylilies and other plants lovingly maintained by the Cassina Garden Club, there stood a remarkable sight: two slave cabins made of tabby, the material of old necessity, fashioned from sea shells mixed with sand and lime. Much better than today's faux stucco.

The cabins had no gutters. Beds of oyster shells ringed the tiny structures under the drip line, like the houseleeks.

And last summer in New England I saw houses that have stood tall since the 18th century. Their gutterlessness was persuasive.

Removal of my gutters was momentous but, alas, unceremonious. I arrived home one chilly January evening to find two men removing the last pieces of sheet metal in the dark. They tossed the remnants onto their truck, removed some mostly decayed leaves from the roof and the walkways and were gone.

For all my determination to ditch the gutters, I felt a little sense of loss. One downpipe near the front porch had supported Carolina jessamine as it twirled toward the roof. I had anticipated seeing this hardy, fragrant vine blooming yellow against the charcoal shingles.

But the gains far outnumber the loss. The house has a sleeker look. Now, when it rains, I can hear the soothing water sounds from all the rooms, as rainwater is not channeled to certain spots. And the sound is clear, unclogged by the fear that the water is transporting wads of leaves that will dam the system as surely as beavers staunch a stream.

And the rain, unhindered, uncollected by gutters, now waters hydrangeas and ferns close to the front porch, as well as nandina, bamboo, pieris japonica and a Japanese black pine planted along one side of the house. And every time it rains it waters my bonsai under the eaves on the side porch.

So far, so good. If the ground gets soggy and threatens the foundation, I can always put in some houseleeks. Or a load of oyster shells.

February 3, 1995

THE REAL THING

Whenever September comes, I think of that line I used to hear television correspondents shout to producers, asking for broadcast time: "Gimme air!"

All summer long that has meant turning on the air conditioner. But now that we are into the months whose names end in "er," I can see natural air in the offing. Gimme air. Real, fresh air.

For me and for plants, indoor and outdoor, real air and plenty of it is a wonderful thing. Like humans, plants suffer illness and discomfort if they are crowded together, breathing stagnant air.

So, for the indoor plants, I turn on the ceiling fans to circulate the air, even if the air conditioner is running. And, outdoors, I prune the trees to allow airflow (and light, too). Tight-growing shrubs, such as boxwoods, get holes pruned in their tops.

Seeking similar increase in air circulation, Lyn and I have had to go to greater lengths. We're changing the windows in our home from the up-and-down kind with the weights inside the frames to the type that opens like a door, controlled by a little crank. The two rooms we have converted so far probably get twice as much air as they did through the old windows.

Making this change has reinforced for us how much we love the feel and sight of air, whether baby breeze or big wind. And the conversion, because it came amid a monstrous heat wave, brought to the surface the conflict between wanting real air and wanting cool comfort. Emotionally, we wanted to throw open our new windows — and some nights we did — but the flesh often is weaker than the heart, and we usually succumbed to comfort, throwing the switch on the AC.

Perhaps our emotional desire for more and more air stems from our effort to bring as much of the outdoors in as possible. In some ways, we are turning the house into a screened porch, compensating for not having a real one. To be sure, watching a plant flutter from a breeze that traveled all the way across the room warms our hearts. It is a healthful bonus for the plant, this air from outdoors — unless, of course, it is air hopelessly fouled.

And, during thunderstorms, opening these tall windows and watching the wind bend pecan and oak trees on nearby streets, then rush to our house, blowing fresh sheets of rain inside, makes us feel like a natural woman and man.

As Lyn said the other day, "Part of the beauty of air is seeing it." But air, like light, is not for everyone. I have known people who spent big money and much time finding and buying excellent homes with great big windows, only to cover them and keep them closed, shutting off both light and air. A friend who did this used to lament her inability to grow houseplants. "If you want plants, you have to change your ways," I told her. She vowed to give light a chance. Air she wasn't too sure about. It was as if letting in something that could have been anywhere outside might open her up to contamination. As if she felt safer with the recycled air.

She would hate our home. Especially in cold weather, when Lyn and I often open windows during daytime and at night set the thermostat way down low to feel the air's crispness, dashing with delight to and from the shower.

Before we get to that chilly point, we will enjoy the seasonal change, as the heavy summer air, laden with reminders of steamy, magnolia-sweet times, gives way to the lighter autumn air, more energetic, unchecked by leaves.

And as the shift takes place, there will be those perfect days that Atlanta gets each year, when the air is neither too warm nor too cold, when breezes rustle dry grasses and big winds shake down a million colorful leaves.

Then, we will throw open our windows and inhale it all.

September 1, 1995

INSIDE LUSH

Throughout the year, I garden indoors as extensively as outdoors, cultivating plant collections that act as furnishings, lending color and texture to various places in the house.

This time of year, though, with the outdoor garden pretty much in bony hibernation, my indoor gardening intensifies. Houseplants get much more attention, as gardening time no longer must be shared with members of the outdoor garden family. I always benefit from this quality time, getting to know the plants more intimately each winter.

The ferns, including Sarah Frond, a zaftig Bostonian with four-foot pigtails, get groomed a couple of times a week instead of every other week or so — the spring and summer schedule. Same goes for the spider plants.

While the indoor plants do not have to compete with outdoor plants this time of year, they must contend with cats. The other day, Buuud, apparently seeking attention, leaped into the center of a rabbit's-foot fern and tried to nest there, like some furry bird. I was impressed that the fern was unharmed, unmussed even. Nice to know how tough they are. And how adroit leaping cats can be. Buuud never even rocked the pot perched on a pedestal.

The African violets bloom their heads off this time of year, in colors from white to deep purple. The least I can do is make sure they have good moisture and a soil line covering their "turkey necks."

Just as violets delight the eyes, sweet olive pleases the nose, blooming all winter. After discovering several years ago that this shrub will flourish indoors, I now grow them in several rooms, where their slightly elusive scent perfumes the air lightly.

One of several snake plants has put up stalks with blooms that should open any week now, releasing more winter fragrance. And a jewel orchid's bloom is about to pop — an occasion so rare in my home that I spend long minutes just staring at it.

Only this time of the year do I water so diligently that the peace lilies never faint. In appreciation, they keep sending up little white flags and putting out new leaves, which get promptly chewed off by Calvin, the eighteen-pound calico given to nervous eating.

Most of the plants need and love winter watering diligence, as they seem to dry out right before my eyes in the season's low humidity. Especially the bonsai, along with the leaf-rich figs and aralias. Only the cacti demand no extra water rations.

Not wanting to spend all this extra gardening time carrying water, I use hydroponics to grow some plants, including pothos, dumb cane, prosperity bamboo, maranta and an African violet.

In, say, a foot-tall glass vase, I put five inches of fine gravel, then a half-inch of horticultural charcoal. Place the plant, roots washed free of soil, on top of the charcoal. Then more gravel, nearly filling the vase and stabilizing the plant. The water level is kept at the charcoal line, with liquid plant food added during the growing season. Over the years, I've even grown small trees this way.

So let winter have its way outside. Indoors, we're growing up a storm.

January 12, 1996

Rose of Sharon

Hibiscus
Syriacus

outside survivor (!)

'China Doll

PART SEVEN

OUT OF BOUNDS

*Like life, gardening sometimes
takes place outside the box*

⌇

DEFYING LIMITS

THERE'S SOMETHING INTENSELY GRATIFYING about pushing limits, whether in gardening or other daily pursuits, large and small.

Boundaries broken in my garden concern plants that aren't supposed to grow here — several that either "belong" in the house or in the tropics, including avocado, oleander and Spanish moss.

I get much satisfaction simply from growing these plants. In addition, they provide reminders about survival, counterculturalism, resilience and the value of raised expectations.

Like folks who carve out identities in strait-laced offices by punching holes in body parts for rings and things, these plant rebels alter the environment, making it more interesting. (Of course, the truly adventurous office workers push limits by shedding suits, ties and heels in favor of comfort.)

Often we test limits consciously, as in marriage (to see if we can live with someone) and divorce (to make sure we can live again).

Then, sometimes, we crash through boundaries without meaning to, as in going into a righteous rage when we feel wronged, thus testing the limits of a relationship or a boss's tolerance.

It was in this spontaneous fashion that I began exploring limits in my garden.

A China doll (Radermachera sinica) was the first — stuck in the ground in August 1989, partly because I had no more room in the house and partly because I wanted to know if this lacy specimen would make it in outdoors Atlanta. It does, dying back and returning annually.

A few months later, I brought home a big hunk of Spanish moss from Savannah and tossed it over the branches of my saucer magnolia.

The moss still drips happily from the tree and actually has spread (or been spread by birds) to nearby shrubs, apparently unaware that it resides about a hundred miles north of the state's "moss line."

Rummaging through fall leaves several springs ago, I discovered an avocado plant that had sprouted from a seed I had stuck in the ground and, like squirrel with acorn, forgotten.

Despite cautions that it was an indoor-only plant, the avocado grew confidently for a couple of winters, reaching about two feet early this year.

Then came last March's blizzard, knocking it down to its roots. Determined, it has returned and is a foot high.

The resilient avocado, together with the other plants, made me a believer in gardeners' ability to dramatically expand our collection of outdoor plants.

To be sure, there are limits. But just as most of us use only a fraction of our mental capacity, it's certain that we're missing many opportunities to grow plants that aren't supposed to thrive in our gardens.

When I first planted indoor plants outdoors, I expected them to be gone after the winter. Later, I raised my expectations, as a couple of "house" ferns also have proved hardy in my garden.

Given the vagaries of weather in these parts, all my rebels may be living on borrowed time, but then, who isn't?

In the meantime, they show the artificiality and arbitrariness of boundaries and the benefits of doing what just isn't done.

Even as we appreciate these lessons, friends, family and I search for explanations of why these plants live in defiance of the rules. It could be the brick wall that surrounds the back garden. But that does not explain the China doll out front.

Or maybe global warming has heated Atlanta.

Maybe. But I prefer believing that these plants, like people, respond to a good pushing of limits. We all need a stretch.

August 20, 1993

THE OUTSIDER GARDEN

A full garden can be a problem, especially if you constantly fall in love with something irresistible — as I do. When a new plant seduces you into taking it home, what do you do with the old plant you must give the boot?

And where do you put the scraggly, the tired, the sick plants while they recover from whatever ails them? And, in a small garden like mine, what happens when some once-prized specimen outgrows the space?

There was a time I'd just give away the healthy excess and toss out the afflicted. Sometimes, if a sick plant was in a pot and salvageable, I'd put it in an area on the side of the house that I called "the hospital." That northside space is shaded and sheltered from harsh winds. It has seen a number of plants survive everything from transplant stress to whiteflies to pruning by cat teeth.

Then, a couple of years ago, I changed my way of dealing with discards; I created an outsider garden, planting beyond the brick wall. That opened up a whole new world of gardening and garden appreciation. But it also has raised anew some questions about the need for walls.

It all began with yarrow. To make space for dwarf papyrus, I ripped out a bushel of this sprawling spreader, which had filled a sunny corner of my back garden. Instead of trashing or composting the yarrow, or forcing it all on a friend, I planted it outside the brick wall, in a super-sunny space alongside the house that had contained only rose of Sharon, irises and daffodils — all planted by the previous homeowners.

That was about three years ago. Since then, I have added dozens of trees, shrubs and perennials to the L-shaped space, which is about three feet wide and runs along the south side of the house and across the back, which faces east.

Miscanthus that had outgrown the inside garden found a home outside, as did three yuccas and a couple of hibiscus whose huge red blooms look better out there. A clump of lamb's-ears moved outside when I tired of seeing it fall sloppily and bloom sparsely in its original location.

Outside, it has thrived. Similarly, I displaced a loblolly pine in favor of a moss garden (which is fast becoming a rock garden, but that's another story). I divided a patch of coreopsis from the original plant and installed it outside about a year ago, and it never missed a bloom.

As I added these plants without plan or timetable, it became clear that something was abuilding; that L-shaped space was starting to look real fine. Serendipity had struck again, as it often does in gardening.

Encouraged by the beauty of the change, I began actually buying plants for the outsider garden, adding two clumps of golden bamboo, two dozen nandina, a Japanese black pine and two pieris japonica.

The result has been a lush welcome from members of the outsider garden as we enter the driveway alongside the house. To family and friends, the outsiders preview what's inside, perhaps making others curious about what is on the other side of the wall. Or curious about why anyone would plant so much outside his wall (fortunately, my property line does not stop at the wall).

And, as the loblolly and bamboo at the back grow taller, they become "borrowed scenery" when viewed from inside the wall. I can look at them and imagine a whole forest of green beyond the wall.

At the same time, the outsider garden increasingly has taken on a character of its own, becoming a distinct space, one that invites lingering instead of just a passing greeting, as was initially the case.

Because they get more sun than most plants in my garden, those on the outside have smaller leaves and tighter forms than their interior counterparts. I suspect they are more drought tolerant, too, because I water them less frequently than the more coddled plants inside the wall.

All this has made me think more about the wall, itself, recalling Robert Frost's poem, "Mending Wall," in which one man believes, "Good fences make good neighbours," while the other notes, "Something there is that doesn't love a wall."

My wall not only separates me from my neighbors; it, of course, separates the outsider and insider gardens.

With people and with gardens, both views expressed in Frost's poem have validity: We all have a love-fear relationship with walls. They give us privacy, even creating enchanted secret spaces. But we know they isolate as well.

Thus, I have a mixed reaction each time I walk along my wall and see an inside-the-wall bamboo shooting new canes outside the wall — or dozens of little roses of Sharon sprouting inside.

Yes, I blame them for breaking into places where I did not want them. But I also hail their spirit for skirting a barrier, trying to be one with another.

April 28, 1995

BEAUTY FLUTTERING

One recent morning, while wolfing down a hard-boiled egg dressed in Tabasco and salt, I glanced up and spied a beautiful butterfly, bright orange, with black and silver spots, clinging to the window.

I stopped in midbite and eased over to the window for a closer look. Transfixed, I just stared. And admired, as the winged creature (a fritillary, perhaps?) warmed itself long enough to allow it to take flight. Soon after it fluttered away, I went to the garden in search of it, but, alas, like so much of nature's beauty, its presence was fleeting, its occurrence unusual.

Abbreviated as it was, the sighting demonstrates the beneficial pleasure of attracting butterflies to the garden. This charming visitor slowed me down, made me stop and note its quiet joy, much the way a garden of plants beckons me to relax, just be.

My fennel plants, recently pruned hard by caterpillars that will become black swallowtail butterflies, testify to my efforts to attract these beautiful insects. My sightings, however, are all too rare — even though hundreds of butterfly species probably roam this area. My wife, Lyn, feeling sorry for me as I crane my neck in search of something other than the small white butterflies, has promised to "import" some large colorful ones for me and introduce them to the joys of life in West End.

Many gardeners need no such help; they have done the right stuff to ensure a steady stream of beautiful, big-winged butterflies of bright hues. And now, the stream flows wondrously. Dog days, yes, these are. But more important, these are the butterfly days, as the colorful fliers zip and flutter, lending grace and beauty to spaces galore.

Dot Farthing of Chamblee has one of these spaces.

In her garden, a wealth of "host" or "larval food" plants including fennel, parsley, dogwood and tulip tree provide food for the caterpillars hatched from butterflies' eggs. When a caterpillar becomes a pupa (the resting stage), then, finally, a butterfly, it feasts on the nectar of butterfly bush, coneflower, lantana, black-eyed Susan and many others. The entire process, from egg to death, is terribly short, about eight weeks on average.

Therefore, we enjoyed while we could, sitting in Farthing's back garden one steamy July morning, sipping sun tea and watching the butterfly show. Orange ones, black ones, little white ones, even smaller brown ones — skippers — whose peripatetic flight patterns illustrate their name. They all entertained and intrigued us with their soaring swooping, their rush to one flower, then another, their long stays when they found just the right sip of sweetness.

"They're so pretty, and they last such a short time," Farthing, a retired art teacher, said languidly. "I can't imagine a garden without butterflies."

Her garden, like many that attract butterflies, also provides space for other wildlife. Surveying the whole — the trees, shrubs, perennials, bird feeders on poles — Farthing portrayed it as a cast in nature's play: "The birds make the music, and the butterflies bring the dance. The squirrels are the clowns."

To be sure, butterflies strike a powerful chord and add dash to a garden. Surely part of their appeal is that they dramatically symbolize total freedom, something so alien to those of us physically or electronically tethered to office and home twenty-four hours a day.

How else to explain the delight and wonder glowing in the eyes of children and grownups alike when we stand in the enchanting glass-enclosed butterfly house at Callaway Gardens in Pine Mountain, Georgia, watching butterflies land on our shoulders, barely rippling the air?

Beyond the visual pleasure, many butterfly aficionados love the thought of enhancing nature while enjoying its fluttering beauty.

Betty Jinright, who heads the butterfly committee of the Garden Club of Georgia, lives and gardens in Thomasville. Her new post means that she will encourage club members to grow plants that provide egg-laying spaces and nectar for butterflies.

Jinright recalls that, as a child, she enjoyed seeing butterflies floating around her grandmother's abelia hedge. Now, she says, she gets "a lot of pleasure knowing that I'm doing something to give them a place to live."

She adds that butterflies are "a real nice learning experience for children," who can watch the short metamorphosis from egg to butterfly.

For some, eggs-cum-caterpillars are not a pretty sight. At Ward's Nursery in Chamblee, Mary Ward Goldenburg, a butterfly lover, sometimes is called upon to reassure her startled customers that the crawling worms on some plants are, in fact, soon-to-be-butterflies. So far, she has resisted putting up signs that say, "Please do not disturb the future swallowtails."

July 28, 1995

NOMAD PLANTS

After years of watching myself move around plants in what could be loosely called redesigning, I began saying, only half-joking, that my plants ought to grow on wheels to make their moves easier.

Of course, plants actually get around fine without wheels; they show up here and there and everywhere in the garden, their seeds borne on air, in water — as well as on and in all all manner of wildlife. They come from near and far, adding serendipity and a taste of mystery to the garden.

Rose of Sharon may be the biggest traveler of all, making it from home outside the back wall to spots all across the back garden — and front, too. Fortunately, Sharon's seedlings come out of the ground fairly easily, providing entire families of new plants for my friends and allowing me to avoid having a garden made entirely of rose of Sharon. Years ago, I planted a little piece of red basil that had hitchhiked home with me in the pot of a shrub I'd bought. Now, it's everywhere, as is the copper fennel that started from a single plant three years ago. Amazing, the fennel seems to prefer cracks in the brick walk to space in the ground, cropping up any place that is sunny. Scotch moss, unable to make it in the back, trekked to the front where it seems happy in sidewalk crevices.

Also, like many gardens I know, mine is populated every year with roaming impatiens, strawberry geraniums and hardy begonias.

The list goes on, growing each year. And with it grows my pleasure. Despite the inconvenience of having to groom some of the travelers out of places I don't want them.

While all these travelers descended from plants I brought to the garden, a separate group has emerged from unknown parents, unknown places. They are the mystery travelers, having arrived from somebody else's garden — or from a wild place near or far.

About three years ago, I noticed the first one, a little holly that sprouted in a sunny spot out front. Soon after, it was joined by another holly sprout out back, then another outside the wall.

Later came a baby spruce, boldly standing next to a full-grown

Japanese black pine, contrasting its blue-green needles with the pine's darker ones.

The trees' close proximity raises questions that often arise in such situations: Does the newcomer get to stay, or is it just in the way? How long can the two coexist before one must go? Is the exotic new traveler more desirable in the garden than the old familiar homeplant? I have not banished any travelers or exiled any old friends. Not yet.

This fall brought a new traveler, ageratum, blooming wild and blue, a festive underplanting for a stately old stand of golden bamboo. Fortunately, the ageratum presents no dilemma; in its new residency it is enhancing without competing.

Among the mysterious travelers, these gifts from the unknown, ageratum is the only one I had never grown in any garden anywhere. Thus, this common wildflower takes on uncommon significance.

Like the others, it invites geographical musing, as it could have come from as close by as the next street or from as far away as, say, New Jersey. Or Texas, or Florida.

They are hardy immigrants, all these traveling plants, bringing their own stories but leaving some tales untold. In getting to know them, I am grateful for whatever I can learn of their histories, personalities, family ties.

Most of all, I love how they beautify and liven up their new space. And how they connect me to their old places — wherever they may be.

November 3, 1995

THE ER PROCEDURE

Please try not to move. If I had a way of anesthetizing you, I would. But I don't. I'll do this as quickly as possible, but you must not move.

With that, I picked up my sharpest blade and began cutting, slicing an eighth of an inch, then a quarter, until finally I had gone in almost half an inch.

Fortunately, the Pfitzer juniper did not move, despite its shaky footing in the spot where I'd just replanted it, despite the rollicking wind gusts on this recent March day.

Good thing. Making one deep cut into the trunk of this beautifully gnarled shrub was bad enough without a slip of the knife making an additional, unintentional gash. But the cut had to be made. At least I felt it had to be.

The emergency surgery was to remove one of those little plastic-covered wires that nurseries use to tie shrubs and trees to stakes in their pots. I've had this juniper about six years and had never noticed my failure to remove one of the little twists. I wouldn't have noticed it ever, had I not moved the plant from its crowded spot in the front garden to an open space next to the wall out back, prompting me to examine the juniper closely. I saw the wire, about six inches above the soil line. It had been there so long, it was embedded half an inch into the shrub's trunk.

After the fifteen-minute procedure, including a thorough cleaning, I checked whether I'd gotten it all. I had.

This was the second such procedure I'd performed in a couple of years. The earlier one was on a Japanese maple.

In each case, I faced the same questions: As the wire is now part of the plant, should I just leave it alone? Or will it do harm if it stays? Will I do harm if I cut so deeply into the trunk? How deep is too deep?

Yet again, gardening was posing risks and trade-offs. Often, in the end, we simply make a choice, not knowing for sure whether it's "right" or "wrong."

I chose to cut.

But not without some trepidation, voiced by Lyn, who had taken a special liking to the juniper in its new home. "I can't believe you're risking Perry's life (she's named it) just for cosmetic reasons," she said after I showed her the white slash under Perry's coffee-colored skin.

Lyn's plaint illustrates the hazard of being married to a non-gardener long enough for her to start having opinions. Next thing I know, she'll be out there moving plants around on her own. She's already brought home a couple, without so much as a consultation.

Of course, Lyn's comment also illustrates the uncertainty I have created in my effort to resolve what, for me, was a problem.

Although I am not willing to call my surgery cosmetic, I concede that even if I thought the plastic would not harm Perry, I still would want it out. There's just something unseemly, undignified about this foreign, unnatural material being buried in something as naturally elegant as a plant. In some ways it reminds me of the pathetic sight of those plastic six-pack holders floating in lakes, waiting to snare an unsuspecting creature. True, no one knows that such a tragedy will occur, but you know in your heart there's a bad chance it will.

So I cut, choosing one risk over another: a deep, maybe fatal cut over a life of ugly indignity, and perhaps plastic-induced illness.

Trying to quell Lyn's concerns and mine, I studied the two-year-old cut on the maple. Its quarter-inch-deep incision has healed substantially, and the weeping tree has not suffered.

If all goes well, Perry will follow suit. I'll believe he's out of the woods when I see new growth. Until then, we watch and wait intensely.

March 15, 1996

COMPOST CROPS

When threats don't work, the surest way to revive a flagging plant or force flowers from a reluctant bloomer is to throw it on the compost pile.

I've seen this gardening principle work countless times. Most recently when I started a compost heap in the corner of the brick wall last year, piling up leaves and twigs and green clippings, throwing in manure and dirt.

If I were a grass grower, I'd chuck in grass clippings, too. I did dispose of my earthworm farm, emptying many hundreds of squiggly composters into the big mix — a move that delighted my wife, Lyn, who had objected to having the worms' large plastic box stashed behind the living-room sofa.

As I watched the compost pile work and sink in the heat, I continued to feed it with vegetable scraps from the kitchen, coffee grounds, egg shells. I threw in shredded newspaper (the worms love it), weeds — and plants that seemed uninterested in living with me anymore, and those killed off by cold.

With spring, there emerged a surprising, familiar set of leaves: spear-shaped, speckled ones belonging to a calla lily I had tossed away for dead, piling cuttings and dirt on top of it. Of course, it bloomed, looking better than it ever had in the garden.

Having seen unexpected resurrections like this for years, I decided that this year, I would intentionally grow plants in the compost pile.

So, back in April, when Sandra and David Wheeles of Suwanee gave me a bunch of tomato seedlings grown at what

Sandra calls their seven-acre "refuge," I put some in the compost pile — the ones I couldn't bear to throw away, although I'd already planted in half-barrels more tomatoes than the law allows. Also, I wedged in a few cayenne and eggplant seedlings.

Soon after I set up my compost garden, Pat Reeve told me about the treasure that volunteered in her Morningside garden in August of last year. The fungi she discovered sprouting in the compost pile turned out to be edible mushrooms. "They were mammoth," says Reeve, who has been composting about seven years. "It was such a surprise. A nice surprise."

Any day now, the mushrooms may return to the compost pile. Meanwhile, Pat has discovered tomato seedlings around her foxglove, growing out of compost that apparently contained tomato seeds.

My intentional compost crops started fast, growing up a storm as I continued to feed the pile with leaves and other yard waste. My first tomato and my first pod of pepper came from the compost pile.

That was just about my last tomato and pepper from the pile. Since I picked those first two, subsequent pieces have been fewer and smaller. And the eggplant didn't even bother to flower.

At the same time, the tomatoes in planters, same kind as in the compost pile, flourished: Better Boy, Early Girl. (Some day, tomato namers should let these children grow up. Better Man. Early Woman.)

The potted peppers and eggplant, too, grow fine. I have to believe that my compost garden withered while the half-barrels produced more 'maters than we could eat green or ripe because another gardening principle kicked in: You can't plan what grows in the compost pile. Just as moss thrives where it wants and refuses to live where it doesn't want to be, compost plants make their own decision on whether to grow or rot.

Sure, you can influence them, planting crops as I did or tacking moss to ground with toothpicks. But this, I discovered, is not nearly as satisfying as my calla lily or Pat's mushrooms.

No, by trying too hard to get compost plants to do your will, you lose the pleasure and surprise of seeing them do their own will, naturally.

August 3, 1996

PART EIGHT

BLIGHTS ON PARADISE

*Once in a while, thorns try
to hide the beauty of the rose*

❧

STOLEN DREAMS

GARDENERS ARE FOND OF saying, rightly, that you almost never find a plant lover who is a bad person. I've always believed that. There's something about connecting with the soil that helps make connections with people, something that makes you want to treat them right.

But we did say almost never. And therein lies a tale. More than one, unfortunately. People who steal what somebody else has invested love and labor in are gardening's secret little dirties.

Wait a minute. I'm not talking about what my mother called "pinching," the time-honored practice of taking a little cutting from a shrub to mark a visit or remember an occasion or place. I'm talking about stealing a plant. In a pot or out of the ground.

Over the years, gardeners have told me of the pain and anger they've felt when their plants turned up missing. One Atlanta friend said several of her potted plants were taken from her porch, only to be offered for sale a few days later by a homeless man hawking them in her very neighborhood. Intimidated by neighbors, he gave back those he hadn't sold.

Several friends who've been victims of plant theft have taken to bolting pots to the porch, along with chairs, or using Sumo-wrestler-sized containers, so big that not even an Olympic weightlifter could make off with them.

And back in the late 1980s, while living in the nation's capital, I was shocked to open the front door to my home on Capitol Hill one morning and see a gaping hole where a rhododendron had lived the night before.

None of this prepared me for the story told me by a woman who lives in Walton County, one of Atlanta's exurban communities — a woman I'll call Joan.

She moved into her home about two years ago and, with her husband providing the labor, began planting the acre-and-a-half lot, ordering shrubs, trees and perennials from mail-order nurseries and buying what she fell in love with on visits to area stores.

"All of a sudden, what I'd planted wasn't there anymore," she said recently. The missing plants she describes are awesome in their range, stolen during repeated intrusions. Ivy, morning glory, wisteria and clematis ripped from an arbor out back. Caladiums, impatiens, chrysanthemums and liriope dug from the ground in front.

During my visit, she showed me spaces between foundation shrubs that she said once contained azaleas. Roses had occupied another empty spot, she said. Juniper, ajuga, carnation, daylilies, daffodils, tulips. The incredible list of missing plants goes on.

"My whole yard has been butchered, and rebutchered and rebutchered," she said sadly. "I feel like I've been violated. Every day I go out into the yard, and it hurts. Your privacy has been violated. It hurts."

The thefts have been "a very exasperating experience," said her husband, adding that he has lost a lot of sleep, rushing to investigate after hearing the dogs barking. "It's hard to get up and work every day, and then watch for thieves every night." He has never caught anyone in the act. And the couple says police officers told them nothing can be done unless thieves are caught in the act.

Admittedly, I was skeptical, never having heard of such extensive garden thefts. But Joan insists that not only did all this happen, but it happened at the hands of neighbors. And she said that part of the pain is knowing that her story is difficult to believe. "I know that what I had in my yard is in their yards," she said.

Why would anyone do this?

"I shared with her, and she shared with me," Joan said of a neighbor. "I don't know why they did it."

She expressed sorrow at losing a sharing partner, but she clearly had not lost the gardener's need to share. Thus, when I arrived at her home, she greeted me with a little box of cuttings and seedlings, mostly indoor plants.

Joan says she has confronted those she accuses, but they deny stealing her plants. Once, she says, she told one person that a certain plant would not survive Atlanta's winters. She says the reply was, "Doesn't matter. It was free, anyway."

The thefts have made her nervous, unable to sleep at times, Joan says. "It's really been depressing. I was a basket case for a while." Gardening, which to most of us is such a freeing activity, now is saddled with restrictions, she says. "I have to think about where I'm going to put something so it won't be stolen. And then where the dogs won't break it."

Estimating that she has lost thousands of dollars worth of plants to theft, Joan says she's never considered taking them back because "it's not worth it." Although "I don't have half of what I bought," she asserts that the money isn't her chief concern. "It's the principle."

Losing the freedom to garden in any spot on your property without fear of having plants stolen must be crushing, something I've never experienced or heard of. Joan's description of it is quiet, measured, as if anger has been beaten down by sadness. At one point, during coffee and cake, she recalled "all the dreaming you do over making your yard beautiful."

And now that the growing season is with us again, "I can't get excited about it. I don't feel the same about it."

But a flame still flickers. She showed me new plantings that include flowering plums, spirea, hydrangea, trumpet vines. "I'm not going to give up yet," she said, as we admired the additions. "But if this year is bad, I will give up."

Let's hope it's a good year.

March 31, 1995

TRASHING THE GARDEN

With hard work and uncommon pleasure, I have created a private world of trees and shrubs and myriad other plants — a world I keep free of hamburger wrappers, soda cans and spent chicken bones.

But I cannot exert the same control or influence in the world beyond my walls and fences. And, unfortunately, it's often filthy out there.

Like anyone who gains appreciation for the environment by simply watching plants thrive and beautify without competition from trash, I resent the encroachment of litter — even litter that is blocks away; the enjoyment of a garden is diminished if the route to it is lined with trash.

Who has the greater right — those who want to throw down

stuff or those who don't want to see it? Should individuals just worry about their own plots and ignore all others? How far does your garden go?

I know which side I'm on. No one has the right to trash my world — large or small. In a sense, all the space around us is a garden, and it deserves respect. Disrespect, like a virus, is catching; one litterer makes others feel it's okay to trash, too. Filth attracts filth, bringing with it a sense of gloom, decay and despair, creating a breeding ground for wrongdoing.

Given my attitude, it is no wonder I have never been comfortable giving handouts to people who solicit amid trash they throw down.

At a traffic light near my home, several such men shuffle forlornly among stopped cars, seeking money or food. Sometimes they hold signs describing their miseries. Sometimes they advertise their willingness to work. The worst are those threatening to squirt water from bottles onto windshields and smear the road grime.

Over the years, Lyn and I have tried various responses, ranging from just saying no to giving a dollar or a can of something to eat. None satisfied us. Then, several months ago, Lyn, "tired of seeing my neighborhood trashed," came up with a better idea, one that I have adopted.

It worked like this recently: I rolled down my window as a man at the corner made eye contact with me. Gesturing toward the candy wrappers and food-to-go cartons that littered his space and the nearby highway slope freshly planted with shrubs and trees, I said as I pressed a few dollars into his hand: "This is your pay for cleaning up this garbage."

"I'll do it," the man said. When I returned home via the same route a few hours later, he had put the trash in a trash barrel, a task too many people apparently seem unable to learn. The corner and the plants on the slope were improved immeasurably — as are Lyn's and my attitudes each time we strike these bargains.

Alas, one corner in southwest Atlanta represents only a fraction of the problem. Countless vacant lots and abandoned buildings invite trash and pollute views. If people litter irresponsibly, who's responsible for cleaning up after them? The city? The property owners?

And why is a neglected house allowed to fall down of its own weight, then just lay on the ground, a giant, rotting heap of trash? There are no rules of civility to prevent this, but are there no laws either? If there are laws, why aren't they being enforced? If these virtual dumps are legal, then the law needs changing.

Until some change comes, it's them against us, the litterers against the nonlitterers.

As a gardener, I will, of course, continue to protect my plants from the indignity of garbage casually tossed onto my space. As a realist I know that governments and some absentee property owners view trashiness with far less concern than I do. But as a dreamer, I will believe that the man on the corner has seen the light and spread the word: The world's his garden, too.

November 10, 1995

MYSTERY FUNGUS

It's not enough that all manner of bugs chomp and nibble at leaves and stems while mildew and fungi scare the life out of entire shrubs and trees. No, that isn't painful enough. For about half a year now, I've been battling some weird organism that's messing with my dirt.

Battling may be overstating the case; what I've been doing is watching in horrid fascination, occasionally digging out chunks of it as it slimes through a section of my front garden, taking over space as it goes.

Back in late spring or early summer, I noticed a patch of ground that always seemed dry. I was trying to grow ferns there, but no matter how often I watered them, they'd be parched the next day. When they died after a few weeks, I dug them out. That's when I discovered what appeared to be a fungus: white, spongy, cottony stuff spreading through the dirt and apparently sucking up the moisture at roots' expense.

I put in more ferns, this time mixing in new, or at least different, dirt. They, too, were killed off. Then I noticed that the thing had spread from the edge of the garden inward about three feet. Digging down about six inches (it travels underground, rarely surfacing), I saw that it had reached an anise, which apparently is mature enough to withstand attack.

I planted yet another set of ferns but treated them like rhododendrons: Instead of digging holes, I set them right on top of the ground and mounded dirt around them.

The tough Alaskan and tassel ferns held on, but I had a feeling The Thing was gathering strength underground and sooner or later would reach up and strangle the unsuspecting plants.

Meanwhile, I reached out to a couple of experts, searching for a way to destroy, or at least contain, The Thing.

So undone was I at having encountered this being for the first time ever in any of my gardens, I must have seemed unbelievable when I told the story of the alien fungus and the murdered ferns.

"So, what kind of fungus is it?" asked the man at the plant nursery, explaining that the type determines what chemical might destroy it.

I told him I didn't know the fungus' name and asked for a "general purpose" preparation. My turning to chemicals was a measure of my desperation, as I don't even use store-bought fertilizer. I bought a liquid fungus fighter, mixed some of it with water and saturated the ground under siege. A week later, the treated dirt did seem somewhat relieved. When I dug into it, it was almost friable.

Since then, however, I have dug again and unearthed my nightmare; the white stuff grinned back at me.

It has not killed the ferns as of this writing. It is as if they are being taunted. Each day, when I walk through the garden, I seek signs of their fate. All seems well on the surface, but I know what lurks down under.

I confided my fears to one extension agent, but I fear the urgency of my situation got lost on the telephone line; you have to see this stuff to respect and loathe it.

"Ummmm, yeah," the agent said. "There've been a lot of fungus problems going around." He quickly changed the subject.

Recently, I was listening to another agent, Walter Reeves of the DeKalb County Extension Service, during his Saturday-morning radio gardening show. Admiring his witty knowledge, I thought briefly of asking Walter to come by and take a look. No. I decided it would be a bad thing if he got contaminated and then infected other gardens, including his own. No telling how this thing spreads.

Nor do I know the organism's origin. Maybe it grew out of a too-thick layer of leaves built up over time. Whatever, I'm watching, warily. Waiting for some fungus-eating bugs to crawl to the rescue. Help is out there.

December 15, 1995

THE BAMBOO WAR

First, I'm going to cut it off. Then, I'm going to kill it.

With those words, inspired by Colin Powell's declaration against the supposedly mighty Iraqi army, I recently launched my war against bamboo.

The object of my enmity is dwarf bamboo, not the tall, willowy reeds whose rustling leaves and grand variety delight and intrigue. Endlessly.

No, my black bamboo, along with my gray and golden must stay — despite the golden's habit of sending up more springtime shoots than there are orange traffic cones around the roads of Atlanta.

The dwarf must go. It was either it or the rest of the garden.

Many plants are considered invasive, but dwarf bamboo is the mother of all invaders. At a furious pace, its plastic-tough rhizomes crawl underground, rooting and shooting across the garden, new stems standing erect like little middle fingers.

I know, I know. I should've known better. When I first planted bamboo about six years ago, gardening friends warned me that it would take over. I've been able to keep my tall bamboo where I want it by simply breaking off the shoots when they grow to about six inches. The dwarf is another grass altogether, as its shoots are much smaller and far more numerous.

If you're planning on planting the small stuff, I'm here to tell you: Don't. Grow it in a pot, as I now do — unless you have infinite space that you want to give to a "groundcover" that will reach more than a foot high. Or unless you don't mind battling millions of unwanted steely shoots.

Yes, dwarf is beautiful. I've enjoyed the way it looked against stones in the front garden and around the fish pond out back. But this year, for the first time, its invasiveness outweighed its beauty. Stunning looks are nothing if they come with a smothering presence.

The dwarf wanted to be the only plant in the garden and set

out to choke out all others, shooting up around any plant within reach. And its reach grew increasingly long over the last few years. By the time I declared war, the three plants I set out had each spread at least fifteen feet, terrorizing everything in their paths — from astilbe to zinnia.

The first few years, I kept up with the new shoots, either cutting or breaking them off. As the numbers multiplied, grooming became more and more difficult.

It's tough seeing a beloved plant go to weed. Struggling with that reality last summer, I declared my dwarf bamboo no longer an accent plant, but rather a groundcover. That got me through the summer, psychologically. But by this spring, the groundcover was covering the plants, too. I was unable to continue rationalizing the dwarf's existence. War was the only option.

And what a war it has been. It began on a weekend, when I dug out each original plant. Then, I pulled out any rhizomes I could. Finally, I went on a search-and-destroy walk over the garden, pruning to the ground any dwarf in sight. Experts say this continuous pruning uses up energy stored in the rhizomes, eventually killing bamboo.

Not since I rid my garden of English ivy a few years ago had I gardened so furiously. Such work seems most difficult, perhaps because it is in some ways antithetical to a gardener's pleasure; I love growing, not ungrowing. But then, ridding a space of invaders pleases, too.

The other plants have exhaled now, but I know I have fought only a battle; the war is yet to be won. Daily, I comb the garden for any dwarf that dares to sprig. When at last I declare victory, maybe in a few years, I hope the bamboo really will be defeated, that it will not be my Saddam.

May 4, 1996

LIFE AMONG THE RUINS

The partially demolished hulk that once was the Sears store at Ashby Street and Ralph David Abernathy Boulevard stands as both an extreme example of urban ugliness and a demonstration of plants' ability to rise above adversity.

For some time now, the site has added a touch of eerie blight to the West End neighborhood in southwest Atlanta, my neighborhood, which includes a wealth of Victorian homes, along with many elegant old oaks and magnolias and other trees.

Many months ago, after the store closed, upbeat rumors began flying: talk of high-rise housing. These rumors may prove true, but they are excruciatingly slow in materializing. After the Sears parking garage finally was torn down, demolition began on the store itself. It advanced at what seemed like brick-by-brick deconstruction, then creaked to a halt. For weeks at a time, a feeble-looking orange and blue crane has sat motionless in front of the semidestroyed store, its wrecking ball at rest.

You'd think there'd be an enforced law against starting, then stopping a demolition project, leaving a building hanging open like those I saw in war-torn Beirut, Lebanon, in 1979.

Driving by, it is a sight to see. Piles of rubble — concrete, twisted steel — stand where cars used to. Broken glass glints sharply from the sidewalk. Hip-hop advertising has sprouted on what's left of the store, including six posters for Fubu jeans, ten for OutKast and six for 2 Live Crew.

Amid all this, plants, shrubs and trees — many of them dismissed as "weeds" and "trash" — thrive, trying mightily to enhance the look of the neighborhood.

Against the abject decay of the building's remains, these disrespected plants seem beautiful, made appealing and apparent in the same unexpected fashion as a mass of wild roses or Carolina jessamine growing around a rotted shack.

To get a closer look, I took a walk around the erstwhile Sears building the other day. In some ways it was like a burned-out forest or a once-verdant hillside charred by volcanic eruption. This site, like any wasteland, was starting over, with new plants of opportunity sprouting here and there, joining old ones that used to landscape Sears.

Along the Ashby Street side of the rubbly hulk a yucca colony stood as it has for years, the plants' spikes leaning into one another. Nearby, the much-maligned trees of heaven grew happily without regard to the disdain they inspire. Several hollies were there, too, lending a strange note of formality to this unfinished chaos.

Twirling through the yuccas and several trees was an incongruous autumn clematis, acting like it was in somebody's back yard.

Naturally, acorns had found their way to the site, producing at least one fine-looking young oak, which went well with the privet growing randomly.

In one section of what used to be the parking lot (its remains had not been hauled off, months after its demolition), a number of small plants with reddish, soft stems and fleshy, azalea-sized leaves grew happily through spaces in the concrete. Purslane, perhaps.

Nearby, morning glories bloomed a purple profusion that put to shame even the best of shows I've had from this wonderful old garden vine. And pokeweed had appeared, as it always does in abandoned sites, its berries darkening, as were those on the pepper vine.

These and other plants, including one that grew seven feet tall and produced lovely yellow blooms, were surrounded by discarded bottles, paper and other trash. They survived that, endured it all, just as they have the seemingly unending demolition.

They shouldn't have to. Nor should the rest of us.

September 7, 1996

A SNAKEY CAPER

A friend was visiting the other day, and as we chatted in the front garden, he happened to glance toward my oakleaf hydrangea. Nearby, under the spider azalea, he noticed something coiled on the ground.

"Is that a snake?" he said.

Yes, it is, I told him. A fake snake. For the squirrels. I explained that several people had told me it would scare away the pests.

My friend, who, like many of us, watches with disgust as the rodents root around his yard, smiled at my snake ploy and told me he takes another tack: "I have a hit man," he said, going on to explain that the shooter gets to keep and eat whatever he kills.

Welcome to the never-ending squirrel war. It is a struggle to prevent these bushy-tailed rats from digging out tender new plantings, pockmocking every inch of ground and biting off tender shoots — a struggle that requires constant vigilance and ingenuity. It also is a struggle no gardener I know has ever won. But, each in our own way, we keep trying. Not every gardener resorts to shooting down squirrels (or having them shot) like the dirty dogs they are, but many think about it.

True, some haven't seen the light. Dee Dyess, a tender-hearted friend who lives in Stone Mountain, coddles the critters. She even had three little wooden houses built for squirrels, complete with shingle roofs that cover them and their feeding dishes. Yes, Dee says, taunting me, "I feed those babies."

Dee. Dee. Please snap out it. Squirrels are not cute, harmless, bushy-tailed babies. They are marauding vagabonds, bad for life. I've seen a whole lot of squirrels with as much gray hair as I have, dragging their tails into my garden to do wrong. They bite tomatoes, decapitate pansies, unearth okra seeds and topple pepper seedlings. They are evil to the bone. Right now, I'm looking at a couple of aging rodents creeping along the high branches of my tulip tree. Now, they're scampering down the trunk. I know where they're headed: toward the little patch of thyme I recently planted.

Maddening scenes like this drove me to the fake snakes.

Hearing they worked, I set off in search of the most realistic ones I could find. At the first store's toy department, I found no snakes at all. Only a few lizards, about a foot long. I snatched them up and resumed my snake hunt.

After futile trips to several more toy departments at stores we once called "five and dimes," I wound up at a shop that sells costumes and gag items. Hooray; they had snakes, too. I picked out a bagful, but not before the salesman treated me to the sight of a fake runny nose and several exciting tales of whoopee cushions, fake vomit and such.

What about these snakes, I asked. Do they really work? Sure do, another store person said, reporting that strategically placed rubber snakes had scared the squirrels right off the roof, across which they used to dash like crazy. As intriguing as fake snakes on the roof were, I resisted more chat and headed home to place mine on the ground — around the bonsai, near the newly planted Corsican mint, amid the still-struggling dwarf mondo. Coiled around the rosemary that mysteriously heaves itself almost out of the ground several times a year — leaving it vulnerable to squirrels delighted to finish the job.

Well, I wish I could report that the snakes work. I can't. Squirrels dig right around them, tossing them aside like so much dirt. The rubber lizards work no better; they're just too heavy to toss.

I think I figured out the problem. These are city squirrels. Never having seen snakes, they have no reason to fear them. I bet a bunch of big fat stuffed cats'll do the job.

June 14, 1997

TELEMARKETERS

Am I ever thankful that tree, shrub and flower merchants have not discovered telemarketing. At least, if they have, they have not discovered my telephone. Getting an unsolicited call from someone selling plants would sorely test my patience, if not my love of gardening.

Am I ever sorry that politicians have discovered telemarketing. Such a painful test it is of my patience with the political process — high-tech candidates usually using automated callers with taped messages bugging us about voting for them. No way does any candidate get my vote after getting a machine to interrupt dinner — without having the graciousness to get on the line in person or put on a surrogate to hear me thank him for the call.

Fortunately, the technology has a little glitch that allows you to tell when a telemarketer — live or canned — is on the line; there's the slight pause after you say hello. Dead air for a second or two.

Then comes the pitch: "This is Arty Blowser. I care about this great city. And as you know, I'm running for office so I can do everything I can to keep it great. I believe I've earned your vote; I hope I'll get . . ."

These days they rarely get that far as I have heard enough of them to recognize the telling pause. Now, if I could only figure out their rings.

I don't know when politicians started this, but they need to stop.

We get breaks after elections, but when they're over, the rest of the telemarketing force will still be with us.

There's the poor guy trying to make a living launching into a spiel about how you can get the best deal ever on new siding for your house. And the myriad callers pushing bank cards with low introductory interest rates — never mind that after six months the rates balloon to the sky.

I can live with them, as they're selling — or trying to sell — what I don't need or want. I have no emotional investment in their pitches.

But what a nightmare it would be to get a call such as this: "Hello, Mr. May? My name is Lisa, and this is a courtesy call on behalf of Tall Tree Greengrowers. Do you have a minute to talk about gardening? You don't? Even if it means receiving a free introductory offer of a beautiful loblolly pine? Free, Mr. May, absolutely free. No obligation at all. Now, don't you want . . ."

CLICK.

So far, gardening salespeople have avoided such nightmarish approaches. There are good reasons they should never succumb to the telemarketing rage, even as it engulfs interests from theater to travel to reading.

While gardeners understand better than most the siren call of a pastime that grows into passion and obsession, we are not keen on pitchmen; gardening, by its very nature, is an act of contemplative discovery, not one to be hawked by hard-selling, fast-rapping strangers. No one can be talked into digging holes for fun. You must find your own way to this sweet imprecise science.

Too, gardening still is relatively low-tech. Certainly, you can spend real big money on fancy equipment, clothes and plants; the current crop of gardening wish books is full of fancy. But you also can garden quite well with the same tools your grandfather used. Given that, gardeners are less likely to tolerate high-tech pitching; it's antithetical to all we dig for.

Similarly, using canned messages to appeal to voters is not political good sense. What it is is disconnected.

November 22, 1997

BLOWING UP A STORM

Noise matters. Anyone who doubts that need only look at the clash over leaf blowers in Los Angeles — a battle that has drawn national attention and counts among its combatants actress Julie Newmar, a leaf-blower hater.

The twelve-year conflict has pitted neighbor against neighbor, quiet-loving homeowner against blower-toting gardener and has led to a city ordinance that ranks among the strongest in the nation; it outlaws use of gas-powered blowers within five hundred feet of residences.

Claiming that banning leaf blowers deprives gardeners (many are poor immigrants) of jobs, the Association of Latin American Gardeners of Los Angeles organized a fast on the steps of city hall to protest the ordinance. No sympathy from Newmar and other celebrities who themselves had spent a lot of time lobbying city hall to get the ban enacted.

Moreover, Newmar distributed antiblower leaflets in her

neighborhood and spray-painted the word "ruido" (Spanish for noise) near a neighbor's house when he refused to silence his Latino gardener's blower. Some opponents deride the leaf blowers as phallic symbols.

The ban, whose implementation had been delayed, was finally approved by the Los Angeles City Council and signed by the mayor. Violators could face fines and fees up to $270, a reduction from original legislation allowing fines of $1,000 and six months in jail.

All this raises intriguing possibilities: What if lots of people in lots of other places rose up against leaf blowers? Imagine, as Newmar's leaflet suggests, hopefully, "the sound of rakes and brooms on a walk or driveway."

The thought takes on increasing significance as late winter approaches; there will be a lot of leaves to get rid of because many of us left them where they fell in the fall. Easy mulch. And now that so many people use blowers not just for leaves but for blowing off grass clippings, too — well, the idea of a leaf-blower backlash is downright delightful.

Easy for me to advocate; I garden on a lot the size of a postage stamp, one of my big-lot friends pointed out when I cheered on the antiblower forces the other day. My retort: Even so, because my neighborhood has so many big old trees, dozens of bags of leaves, acorns, blooms and other tree droppings fall on that little plot every season.

To be sure, a leaf blower's mighty tempting. In fact, I bought one several years ago, an electric one with a long, orange cord. Used it a few times, even. I gave it up for a very simple reason: Noise matters.

I just couldn't stand listening to the din. And the gasoline machines are even noisier than mine, which now languishes in the shed. The deafening racket is bad enough if you're behind closed doors and windows. But if you venture outside, it's absolutely assaulting, like loud music and raggedy mufflers. Long after using the blower, I'd hear it roaring in my ears.

So, I went back to rakes and brooms. And hands in spots too tight for storebought implements.

That was long ago. My brief fling with a leaf blower brought home to me how soothing a rake and broom can be. The steady strokes, the easy scraping, are natural, gardenlike. Too, like watering with a hose, raking the ground puts me in close touch with individual plants and with the garden as a whole. Raking is a caress, leaf-blowing an attack.

Nevertheless, I understand that some people make a living blowing leaves and grass and dust. I understand the concern of all who don't want a ban on leaf blowers to put them out of work. I have a solution: Let them get rakes.

January 10, 1998

A DEATH IN THE HOUSE

The noise was slight, muffled, but noticeable in the quiet house. At first, I thought it was a cat stumbling; they're not nearly as sure-footed as they pretend to be. A look around showed all three of them sprawled asleep on the bed upstairs, as they are wont to be through most of the day.

Downstairs, I looked around, finally finding the sound's source in the dining room. There lay the entire top of my large jade plant, like a sleeping cat, on the floor next to its container. All that was left in the big black Japanese pot was a stump, standing just an inch above the top of the soil.

Losing a longtime member of your plant family always saddens. But there's something extra tough about losing a houseplant this time of year — when indoor greenery takes on added significance as so many outdoor plants hunker down for the winter.

The jade was not pushed; it fell. A quick look at the stump and the broken end of the fallen top showed serious decay. It reminded me of a rotted tooth in the mouth of the bluesman whose rocking and reeling I enjoyed till dawn in a juke joint near Augusta, Georgia, many years ago. As gone as that jade's trunk was, it's amazing it didn't fall sooner.

Now that it had, it brought me down, too. I picked up the remains and put them by the front door to let them lie until my next trip to the garbage can — or the compost heap.

Neither end seemed fitting. I placed the jade top in the tall Chinese vase in the front parlor — so that it appeared to be growing out of the vase's top, cascading down its side. I thought it looked pretty good. Lyn didn't.

"Is that jade on it's way to going someplace?" she asked sarcastically.

"No, that's its destination," I answered.

"Under the mistaken assumption that it's attractive?"

"I f-e-e-e-l your disdain. But it doesn't have to be that way. To appreciate this jade, where it is, you must have a willing suspension of disbelief. It's not dead; it's just being transformed."

Well, it's been a more than a week since the jade fell down. So far, Lyn has not tossed it while my back was turned. And, it remains alive-looking, sitting atop that vase. I know that sooner or later decay will finish the jade, that it'll have to go.

Until then, I'm taking the time to get used to not having it in front of that sunny window, where it had been for years. And, I'm trying to decide whether to harvest a few fleshy leaves from it, cut off a stem or two, for propagation, to keep this old jade alive.

Old in my experiences with jades, over the last dozen or so years I've lost too many to remember. They'd stay alive for a few months, then turn to mush and collapse. Jades have always been among that group of plants that are supposedly easy to grow. But not for me; they've always been difficult, as have snake plants.

My fallen plant was my first jade success; it had grown so fine since I bought it at the Atlanta Botanical Garden gift shop about five years ago. Fine enough to make me believe my jade jinx was over. The happy jade, in combination with the several snake plants that have survived for years, signaled an end to my long difficulty with so-called easy-to-grow plants, I thought.

Now, I'm back where I've been. What was easy a week ago is difficult again. And I'm wary. Will my apparently satisfied snake plants, with me for as long as the jade was, turn to brown mush and fall to pieces?

I should have known better: As long as I've gardened, I ought to know that, as easy as plants are to read most times, they sometimes suffer without a sign — laughing on the outside, dying on the inside.

January 24, 1998

Saintpaulia ionantha ~
named for Baron Walter von St. Paul.

Propagated by
leaf cutting ~

~ African Violet ~

PART NINE

SHARING PRECIOUS MEMORIES

*With each plant, every talk,
lives mingle, growing together*

∾

SWAPPING AND BEGGING

BROWSING THROUGH AN EAST Point, Georgia, antique shop, I came upon a couple of big old plants stashed among the chests, mirrors and tables: a pencil cactus and a crown of thorns. Uh-oh. Goodbye browsing, hello begging.

It had been fifteen years or so since I last grew either of those, I told Sara Goen, the shop owner, and since they both needed pruning, well, how about a couple of clippings?

Sure, she said, producing a pair of scissors. Then, as I was leaving, I opened my mouth to thank her, only to have her hold up both hands. "No," she said. "Never say 'thank you.' It's bad luck."

I knew that. My mother had told me that many years ago. Just as she had told me that plants should never be bought; they should be given. Or traded. Or "pinched," her term for breaking off a piece.

A week after getting my two clippings, I returned the favor, taking Goen a piece of one of my cacti. We thus had completed one of the enduring traditions among gardeners, indoor and out. In our exchange, we were increasing our own stock and at the same time passing it on. All without cash.

"The barter system was in place before there was ever any money," says Tommy Irvin, Georgia commissioner of agriculture, calling today's plant swapping simply a variation on the old practice of, say, trading corn for flour or soap.

Swaps also accomplish something much more satisfying. They act as bridges to our past, connecting us to people and places that might be long forgotten if not for these living, growing reminders. As they multiply and mature, they become like a closetful of children's clothes in ever-larger sizes, charting the years.

Irvin's wife, Bernice, is the family plant trader, counting peonies, a rose and an orange among plants she has been given.

Like human family trees, plant genealogy can take many twists and turns. Mrs. Irvin got a rose clipping from her daughter-in-law's mother, who had gotten one from a neighbor. Who knows where the plant first took root?

Plant bartering takes almost as many forms as there are plants, including exchanges stemming from home visits, advertisements and chance encounters.

Neighbors and I have traded plants for years after spying something appealing in one another's gardens during periodic yard chats. On several occasions, I have gone on binges of garden redesign, ripping out plants and hauling them off to friends, who have in turn loaded me down with as many plants as I brought.

A few years back, while waiting in a store checkout line, a woman and I started talking plants. I wound up accepting her

invitation to view her garden immediately and take clippings —
no doubt startling her husband, who could not have expected to
see a stranger rummaging among his oak-leaf hydrangea.

Whenever you make a trade, you make an acquaintance. And
plants enhance memories of people and places, replaying them
like nature's videotape.

Goen had admired her mother's "old-time lavender rose,"
flourishing in Fairmount, Georgia. Wanting one of her own, she
made thirteen cuttings and planted all of them. One took root.

That was twenty-five years ago. Since then, death has taken
her mother, but the rose — and through it vibrant family memories — lives today.

I have shared a trailing African violet over and over after
receiving it eight years ago from Penny Pagano, a friend who lives
in Washington, D.C.

Spreading the plant wealth around this way has a practical
side. After I gave my daughter Leslie a leaf from one violet, my
original plant decided to die on me. But, like someone claiming
insurance, I was able to go back to Leslie and get a leaf from her,
keeping the family violet going.

For practicality, or just plain pleasure, many of us are sharing
as fast as we can. Goen at the antique shop says I wasn't the first
to get pieces of her plants. "Sharing plants is something from way
back," she says. "It's an innate thing. People like plants and want
to share them."

Usually you know who did the sharing, but about a year ago,
I opened my front door to find a rabbit's-foot fern in a little pot,
sitting on the porch. No note, no telephone call from the giver.

If you're the one, rest assured the plant's doing fine. But do
speak up. Since we last didn't talk, I've put in a lot of plants, and
I'm ready to share.

May 21, 1993

PUBLIC HOUSING BLOOMS

When I met her, she was pruning in the rain, a sure clue that Mary Stalling was born under a gardening sign.

She confirmed that soon after our first handshake, saying gardening "comes from my roots. My grandmother had flowers. I try to recapture my childhood flowers in my garden, because I feel they are the flowers of Atlanta."

Azalea, forsythia, hydrangea, mahonia and rose are among the many reminders of youth thriving in Stalling's front yard. Fledgling veggies in the back include corn, bell pepper, carrots and tomatoes. As she put the finishing snips to a neighbor's holly, Stalling talked about what her gardening life is like in Joel Chandler Harris Homes, a public housing complex on Ashby Street in southwest Atlanta. Her six-apartment building has caught my eye and many others for years, as it blooms mightily each spring and otherwise delights throughout the year.

"A lot of people come by here and say, 'I want flowers in my yard, too.' I give away oodles of flowers," said Stalling, a homemaker for her four grandchildren. (Before I knew it, she'd uprooted a mysterious perennial and pressed it into my hands.) "People stop and holler and say it looks good. When the stoplight catches them, they always look over here."

Nevertheless, she has heard the stereotype of dreary life in the barren projects, and she combats it. "It's a myth that we don't garden," she said. "An apartment is an apartment. Home is what you make it."

That attitude has made the highly visible row of apartments on Ashby notable to the point that it has been mentioned on a radio show and filmed by students from nearby Atlanta University Center as an example of a public-housing home made beautiful.

"People always say it doesn't look like government housing," said Stalling, a five-year resident.

But increasingly, it does. Officials from the Atlanta Housing Authority, county extension services and the Atlanta Urban Gardening Program cite rising interest in gardening among residents of the city's Forty-five public-housing sites, which are home to some thirty-four thousand residents. Among the results, experts say, are a heightened sense of community, relief of stress and increased self-esteem.

"Garden clubs are springing up in many of the complexes," said Cynthia Hoke, spokeswoman for the housing authority, adding that growing food and flowers "gives people a sense of pride." "Some people say the gardens reduce crime," said Robert Brannen, a Fulton County extension agent for fifteen years, "because when you have a community garden, people keep an eye on it."

Crime-stopper or not, he said, "when you've got pretty flowers and tomato plants, then you own that. You and it are a part of each other." As for the incidence of gardening in public housing, he said, "I think it's a lot more common than people think."

Bobby Wilson, director of the Atlanta Urban Gardening Program, said his office provides technical assistance to clubs in about a dozen public-housing communities in Fulton and DeKalb counties. The office receives half a dozen new requests for help each week.

Stalling and her neighbors have been deep into flowers for years, crediting longtime resident Mary Askew for starting it all. Their ornamentals are what you see from the street, as everybody's vegetables grow out back or on the side. Not a formally organized group, the residents of the six apartments have developed into a closely knit gardening community.

On a recent day, several residents were drawn outside by the perfect spring weather. There was some digging, some planting, grass-cutting, raking and a bit of garden banter, including the well-known gardener's habit of playing down one's own ability.

"I tell Miss Mary there's no way I can keep up with her," said James Fears, a retired mechanic who has lived in the complex since 1975 and suffers from arthritis and a bad leg.

Despite his protestations of ineptness, Fears has managed to keep the same patch of collards going for two years, showing them off now as a novelty. Beans and tomatoes are planted. His ornamentals seem to be doing fine, too (holly, azalea, iris, hosta, juniper, dusty miller), although he said his late wife was the real gardener.

So what's up with this stuff about the "project mentality"?

"Just because you live in public housing, you don't have to have your place all littered up," Fears said. "You got to keep your place up as though you own it. It'd look bad for people to pass and see the yard full of paper and bottles. Yes, it's work in it, but I enjoy doing it."

Another neighbor, Emma Prather, uniformed and hurrying off to take her post as a school crossing guard, agreed, indicating that there's no big mystery as to why she and her neighbors garden. "I just like a beautiful place," she said, noting her partiality to azaleas. "I care about where I stay."

Meanwhile, Stalling had put her grandchildren to work, and they seemed to enjoy it, too, running the lawn mower and raking up grass while Stalling weeded her white azaleas.

Said Stalling: "People see these flowers, and they say, 'Somebody lives here.'" And loves what a garden can do for life.

April 15, 1994

THE AMAZING GRACES

Buford, Georgia — They are like two sisters with the same name: Grace.

They get along so well that many birth sisters would envy them. No harsh words, hurt feelings or bruised egos intrude on their friendship, which has lasted thirty years — or is it forty? Time seems only a number when they discuss their history. Suffice it to say they've known and loved each other a long, long time.

The world could take a lesson in racial harmony from the two Graces, Grace Harris, who is black, and Grace Holland, who is white. Both eighty-one years old, born a couple of weeks apart, they live only a couple of miles apart with husbands (Cleve Harris and E. J. Holland) who also get on just fine. They seem to have achieved what all of us should seek in our contacts with someone of another race: a relationship in which skin color is only a physical feature, not an indicator of worth or compatibility.

Because the two women seem so oblivious to race in a society that makes so much of it, I feel a little strange mentioning it. But at a time when widespread racial harmony seems a distant dream, it seems right to take a look at the togetherness that blossoms in a little community in Georgia.

During my visit with the two Graces (known as "the Amazing Graces"), they were much more comfortable talking about their colorful flowers than about their colorblind relationship; for them the most important thing about color is what it looks like in the garden. That is the natural way things should be.

It was gardening that first brought the Graces together. And it is gardening that glues their relationship, just as it does countless others the world over.

"Flowers," they say together, matter-of-factly, when asked what has kept them together so long. They describe each other as "caring" and "sharing" and "lovely," discussing their work together to provide blooms to area churches and clubs.

Looking at both gardens, you see the same plants, many of which started in one or the other and were shared: Jerusalem cherry, begonia, azalea, ginger lily, canna lily, day lily, burning bush, cypress vine, rose of Sharon, four-o'clocks, roses, dahlias, trees galore and so much more.

For all their similarities, the Graces do have differences. Harris is a huge talker, while Holland is not. At least, she is not while the two are together. Also, despite their growing the same plants, their styles differ.

Harris explains it this way, her words pelting the air like a snare drum as she ably leads a walk through her garden, despite failing eyes and lingering injuries from two accidents: "Let me tell you something about Holland; she is a lady who loves perfection and big blooms. Now, I'm interested in landscaping. She doesn't grow anything unless it's a big giant. We used to help decorate the church. She had some dahlias. They were so big I had to make slingshots to hold their heads up. Anything you got to tie up, that's not my thing. But she grows giants."

Says Holland, softly, a saxophone to Harris's snare: "I don't have any rhyme or rhythm. I just stick out things without much of a plan."

Plan or not, each gets to the same beautiful gardening place. And their mutual admiration of each other's spaces meant almost daily visits during most of their friendship.

"That's one thing I miss about driving," Harris says. "If she had anything blooming, she'd call me and I'd run over there and see it."

There are fewer visits by car since Harris's October auto accident, followed by a December fall that broke her hip and several ribs. But, says Holland, who does not like to drive, "We stay on the telephone."

On this day, though, they are visiting together at Harris's garden and enjoying it immensely, chatting about . . . flowers, naturally, as we walk.

Harris: "She gave me ginger lilies. I get a hankering for the old stuff."

Holland: "Don't forget to root me some of those impatiens."

Harris: "No, I haven't forgotten."

On race, Holland says they truly don't understand what the fuss is about. Harris says people in Buford were "one big family" even before integration, asserting that she suffered more racism during a visit to Pennsylvania than ever in Georgia — where a Buford park was named for her in 1989, honoring her gardening gifts to the community.

The Graces' well-known colorblind friendship is inspiring, says their gardening friend and protege, Mary Marx, describing them as "just two girls who love each other and and love their gardens."

At one point during our stroll around the one-acre lot, Holland lovingly puts her arm around Harris, steadying her on the path lined with ferns and wildflowers. Says Harris, apologizing for not having spiffed up her grounds, "You've never seen my woods look like this."

"No, no, it doesn't look bad," Holland says, patting Harris's shoulder.

Not bad at all. In fact, it looks real fine. Just like their friendship.

September 22, 1995

GROWING KNOWLEDGE

From time to time a lot of us preboomers sit around and talk about how young children, and some older ones, have no earthly idea about where food comes from.

It's not unusual to find a child who looks at a huge, ice-cold watermelon without knowing it began as a tiny seed. Or one who chomps into a handful of peanuts, thinking they grow on trees.

Children like this are disconnected in a way that goes way beyond food-growing; they are at risk of losing touch with nature itself, with other people — and with themselves. Such losses would create problems for all of us.

That is why a brief chat with a little girl in a bookstore in the Atlanta suburb of Alpharetta so warmed my heart.

It was last Saturday night. I was signing books, and she was browsing through them. She looked about eight years old but clearly was an old soul, wise and knowing way beyond her years. After a minute of general chat about gardening and books and how she had come to the store with her father to look for a Mother's Day gift, she began talking about her own gardening experiences.

She and her mother grow food together, she said, in several spaces containing a grand variety of vegetables. We talked about how plants like tomatoes and peppers bloom and how, as the blooms fade, they are replaced by little tomatoes and peppers. Her matter-of-fact tone was laced with knowledge and wrapped in the delight she clearly gets from gardening.

Our conversation was over in just a few minutes, but its impact lasts.

With television, video games, skating lessons, dance classes and myriad other activities available, it is good to know that a parent and child still find time to share a garden.

In addition to the obvious payoff in food and fun, children and mothers and fathers find all manner of experiences and lessons in backyard plots. If you garden long enough, you'll see a lot of life: birth, growth, nurturing, love, happiness, heartbreak, death.

Not only do these experiences teach; they can connect, too.

The girl in Alpharetta has eyes that look alive. Hers are not the dead eyes that you too often see staring hollowly from so many young, immobile — hostile, even — faces these days.

The dead-eyed and disconnected affect us all, even if we do not know them. They are the ones who often litter, disrespecting society's garden by throwing hamburger wrappers and soda cans onto the ground wherever they finish eating and drinking. As they grow older, they toss them out car windows, along with their cigarette butts. Such actions breed crime, as filth for some reason makes bad people feel it's okay to do wrong.

On the other hand, every gardening child I've ever known has had a healthy respect for the earth, caring about what belongs on it — and what doesn't. No trash. I cannot imagine the girl from Alpharetta tossing a candy wrapper into somebody's yard.

Closer to home, Kalen, the three-year-old daughter of neighbor friends Vicky and Tony Axam, is another good example of how respect for the Earth can develop at an early age.

Vicky, who gardens as time allows, always has instilled in Kalen and her younger sister, Karaz, the need to keep the earth looking good, free of debris. During a recent drive, Kalen saw some walkers throw down trash, prompting Vicky to say that such behavior "makes the earth sick."

Later, when she saw someone throwing trash from a car, Kalen said, "They are bad, and they need to go to time-out."

She, like the girl from Alpharetta, is wise beyond her years. We need more like them. Before the sickness overcomes us.

May 18, 1996

TO BORROW A VIEW

All your garden doesn't have to be in your garden. Some of us like to use our neighbors' trees, shrubs and such for background pleasure. Call it borrowed scenery. Or borrowed landscape.

Blanche Foley and I talked about our love of this kind of borrowing as we toured her Atlanta home recently. A prolific writer of garden verse, Foley explains her largess in "The Borrowed Landscape."

> *I use my neighbor's house every day,*
> *And as to this loan, she has no say.*
> *Especially in the winter when spring won't seem to hatch.*
> *Her house looks like Mount Vernon, and mine looks like Dogpatch.*
> *So I borrow her trees and her lawn and her flowers.*
> *From my back sun parlor I steal them for hours.*
> *They're mine for the day, just for a lark.*
> *I give them back only at dark.*

Praising her neighbor's pansies, dogwoods, hollies and "negative space" of manicured lawn, Foley says, "It's always perfect over there. It's the orderliness I like."

Foley modestly plays down her own space; its lovely plantings of viburnum, dogwood, magnolia, camellia, nandina, mahonia, spirea and cherry make it a long way from Dogpatch. But she knows that no matter how much you love your own garden, you can always profit from the plantings in someone else's.

Japanese-style gardens routinely borrow scenery, including hedges, trees, hills, valleys, lakes, the sea, to connect a space to the world beyond while at the same time retaining privacy and seclusion. Borrowing scenery, which can make a small garden seem larger, is best done by framing the borrowed scenery with something on your own property, such as a window (making the term "picture-window" truly apt), tree branches or a gap in a row of hedges.

At almost an acre, Foley's triangular-shaped corner lot, is not small. She borrows more out of pleasure than need for illusory expansion. My much smaller garden is enlarged by my borrowing several of the trees on neighbor's lots. Pecan trees framed by windows add strong scenery to my back garden. The front is enhanced by the pre–Civil War oak viewed through my office window.

Scenery was not planted specifically for Foley and me to borrow, of course. But if you have a cooperative neighbor or an empty, available lot nearby, you might just plant something you can then borrow. As Foley noted when she handed me a hunk of one of her plants at the end of our visit: "If you don't have room for this iris, plant it in a neighbor's yard. Then you can look at it."

Well, I found room for the iris inside my garden, but I have made several other plantings in the neighborhood courtyard, and I can view them beyond my back garden wall. These plantings all happened to be evergreens, allowing lush enjoyment in every season — although decidious plants can lend a striking quality to the landscape with their elegant bare forms.

I planted a juniper that was outgrowing its pot, and now it has room to stretch out, still good-looking from across the way. Similarly, the golden bamboo for which I had no room inside the wall now waves and whistles in the wind outside the wall, becoming — visually — a part of the garden it left. The loblolly pine that needed more space than was available in the front garden now peeks over the back wall, part of the mid-range borrowed scenery, a welcome tie-in between the garden and the big old pecan trees way beyond.

In some ways, these moves amount to borrowing from myself. Whether we borrow from one another's plantings or from our own, the result is the same; our gardens gain. And thus do we.

January 25, 1997

PART TEN

PLACES

*Large and small, each one
grows life in ways special*

∾

BEAUTY AMID BATTLE

WASHINGTON — COMING BACK TO this town, where I worked and lived for about ten years, has its rituals. They include a long, languid meal at an Ethiopian restaurant on 18th Street. A sushi lunch orchestrated by Kawasaki-san at his bar on 19th Street is a must, too.

And in this city of rituals, one of my most pleasing is a visit to the Capitol grounds, where trees and shrubs, discreetly labeled, along with colorful seasonal flowers, complement the stately elegance of the domed building.

The botanical garden, a short walk downhill from the Capitol, and the arboretum, a quick drive away, draw crowds of plant lovers; that is their job. But the grounds of the Capitol please and soothe in a different way — much like a garden that captivates without trying.

So it was on a Saturday in mid-December, the day much of the federal government began its longest-ever shutdown, the second closing last year. The grounds were beautiful, as always, but that beauty served as a counterpoint to the sad and ugly budget battle featuring Bill and Newt and other Democrats and Republicans — a shortsighted, unstatesmanlike wrestling match that crippled so much of the federal city, angering and frustrating visitors like Lyn and me.

Still, there was the beauty. Like the republic, it endures, let us hope. The beginning of a new year is a time of hope, isn't it?

As Ronald Reagan's image makers realized when they moved his inaugural ceremonies to the Capitol's west front, that side of the building is the most visually pleasing, as it opens onto a view of the Mall and the monuments.

I don't know if the image people thought about it, but that side also is where the plantings thrive splendrously.

Starting on the House side of the Capitol, we admired Canadian hemlock and Japanese larch. Oblivious to the goings-on under the dome, these trees invited touching and close looks on this mild afternoon. And right next to the Capitol steps, magnolias stood sentry, gazing at the gaily dressed Christmas tree just down the way.

Walking north, toward the Senate side, we passed people and squirrels. There seemed to be more of the latter. And Lyn noted that they were so much fatter than the squirrels back home in Atlanta. Maybe the Capitol rodents grow corpulent on all the pork coming out of the building, I speculated.

To be sure, the senators and representatives apparently were dishing it out as we spoke. A man walking by told a couple of companions, "The government shut down, but Congress exempts itself."

Disdainfully, both the Congress and the White House went about their business, while the museums (but not some money-making museum shops) and various departments were stopped

— despite outcries from around the nation and murmurs from federal employees, like the Museum of American History employee who spat, "A pox on all their houses."

Still there was the beauty. Tucked into the grounds of the Senate side is my favorite Capitol feature: the Grotto, a lovely space designed by architect Frederick Law Olmsted and built between 1879 and 1881.

The red brick structure, with tile roof, wrought-iron gate and intimate seating areas, beckons, like a secret garden. It feels like a combination of Asian, biblical and medieval; cozy like a cave, it is at once calm, spiritual, mysterious.

Surrounding the Grotto are trees, including hardy orange and sugar maple, along with a profusion of mondo, azaleas, pieris, aucuba, mahonia and ornamental grasses.

This old, earnest beauty made the ritual visit the right thing to do. While I will never forget the contrast between the living Capitol grounds and the dead government on that December day, I enjoy knowing this new year is an election year.

And when the bickering pols are gone, the beauty will be there still. That's one thing they can't shut down.

January 5, 1996

A MARVELING VISITOR

Atlanta — Beauty that we've come to know often is enhanced when seen through someone else's eyes. No matter how much we love a home, a garden, a person, we do grow accustomed to their presence, thus running the risk of taking them for granted.

Having a visitor praise our loves can energize our own appreciation, as if we're seeing them for the first time.

So, too, it is with a city.

Visitors marvel at Atlanta's remarkably varied communities, increasingly including people from around the globe. With more neighborhoods than we can count, this area offers architectural styles for just about everyone — from Victorian to Tudor to Colonial and Greek Revival and more. Shotgun houses and antebellum ones recall bygone eras as surely as myriad apartment complexes and condominiums mark the present.

Just as the city's archictectural diversity appeals visually and emotionally, its greenness strikes a chord, always. Like visitors, I am always moved by the sight of so many trees whenever I ride a plane over the Atlanta area. Still so many, even after all the clear-cutting for new building.

As much as I understand and appreciate what greenery does for the soul, I was not prepared for the depth of passion that Kathryn Hill voiced on her visit to Atlanta earlier this month.

"Absolutely stunning" is how she described the city's plant life. Hill, who lives in Fairport, New York, and was here for a weekend to teach a computer course, says she drove her rental car around the city and found one treat after another. The pink blossoms on cherry trees delighted her with their delicacy and surprised her with their timing, as nothing was putting on such a show in her town. Pansies, too, caught her eye, as did daffodils.

"You live in the best of worlds for gardening," Hill told me Sunday, during dinner at Blue Ridge Grill.

She's right, of course. Despite the late winter freezes and the endless summers, Atlanta accomodates a broad range of plants — unlike places that never get cold or those that stay warm for just a New York minute.

Our conversation started me thinking about how much fun it is to drive through neighborhoods from Cherokee County to Fayette County, as I do, routinely, enjoying spaces that gardeners are having fun beautifying. Too, I noted how inspiring it is to walk the grounds of the Atlanta Botanical Garden and the Atlanta History Center. And how the Southeastern Flower Show each year primes gardeners to dig in the dirt with gusto.

In 1989, when I returned South for my second time around as an Atlantan, I noticed many changes, including the blossoming of restaurants (when I lived here in the 1970s, people used to joke that going out for an exotic meal meant grabbing a takeout pizza) and of business buildings — once dominated by unlandscaped utilitarian glass towers, now characterized by structures that try to outdo one another with distinctive tops ranging from wondrous to whimsical. And, as the elegant landscaping at Hotel Nikko and NationsBank Plaza proves, gardens dress up business buildings real well.

All of this makes Atlanta look smart to visitors like Kathryn Hill. She sees a lot of cities, as her work and personal travels take her all around America. Atlanta stacks up beautifully.

"I love this city," she said. "It's such an exciting city. This is February, but in my mind it's northern February, when you're not going to see blooms like those here. It's amazing; it makes me believe spring is coming."

It is coming, Kathryn. It is. And if you think Atlanta's cutting up now, you ought to see it then. Boy hidy.

February 22, 1997

GREENING OF GOTHAM

New York — The sign in the huge street planter way downtown on West Broadway was crystal clear and a little bit plaintive: "Wildflower seeds planted. Please don't walk or pee on me. Let me live. No dogs. No bikes."

In midtown, on Lexington and Madison and 5th, no signs mark the spots outside the elegant stores, and plantings proliferate: hemlocks, impatiens, ginkgos by the dozens. Uptown, on Madison at 100th, shrubs and flowers galore grace the modest, massive George Washington Carver Houses, including Japanese maple, lilac, rose of Sharon, yew, viburnum.

This is the New York that few visitors acknowledge. The green, nature-hungry New York. Yes, a tree grows in Brooklyn, and a whole lot of them grow in the Borough of Manhattan, too. While the odds may seem daunting, the truth is, the city's rough environment is handily overcome by the will and desire of New Yorkers to maintain the civility that grows with plants.

Despite the vast greenness of Central Park, most portrayals of Manhattan center on its noise, grime and alleged rudeness. The city is about as noisy as I remember from my time here in the early 1970s at Columbia University's Graduate School of Journalism. But the grime is diminished greatly in the 1990s in much of Manhattan, where streets are cleaner, garbage is wrapped tighter and dog owners have learned to clean up after their pets.

As for rudeness, I never felt it as much as some say they have. During the time I lived here and on numerous visits, I've seen young people on buses give up seats to their elders, residents give directions to lost strangers. And shop clerks actually saying, "Thank you" to customers. When Lyn and I visited recently, all that was still happening.

The plantings add an even greater note of civility. As a native of the South, where the growing is easier and the space greater, I have always marveled at the New Yorkers' determination to garden in cramped, unembracing places. I understand that determination. More than two decades ago, I lived in a student-housing apartment with so little light, even pothos couldn't live. I tried it anyway. Now, our daughter, Petria, newly graduated from Columbia Law, is equally determined and more successful — growing her first plant in her sunny East Village apartment: pothos.

It's good to see that cut flowers still light up produce stands all over town. And entrepreneurs with truckloads of tropicals still set up shop on street corners.

I've noticed that Manhattan's old quest for the green has been joined by cutified businesses selling everything from baby herbs to weathered clay pots. These shops have popped up with almost the same vigor as the book- and coffee-store combinations. And with the same civilizing result.

None of this is to say that New York's green streets shield you from a New York moment. We had several:

• In the middle of a 5th Avenue crosswalk, Lyn and I passed The Donald walking in the opposite direction. Two men in front of us had this exchange:

"Hey, that was Donald Trump."

"Yeah, I started to ask him, 'Who are you (sleeping with) now?'"

• At the Museum of the City of New York's wedding clothes exhibit, a guard asked each visitor if we'd marry the same person again. So far, thirteen of sixteen had said no, she reported with great mirth.

• Trying to brush off an American street beggar, I said, in Spanish, that I didn't speak English. Undaunted, he hunched his shoulders, extended both hands palms up and said: "Señor, señor. Por favor."

All this and green streets, too. I'm not saying I-I-I-I love New York well enough to live here, but it's sure nice to visit.

May 31, 1997

CALL OF THE MARSHES . . .

McIntosh County — For more than thirty-five years, ever since I was a boy soldier at Fort Stewart, I have regularly visited the Georgia coast — enjoying seafood virtually every meal and reveling in the area's many natural charms.

Among them are the live oaks, of course, trees that resemble giant bonsai dripping Spanish moss like so many old gray beards, conjuring memories of mysterious nights and miserably hot days. But pungent, sensual. Too, there are the marshes, lushed by grasses waving in the breeze, rising and falling with the tides.

As much as anything, the marshes epitomize the coast. As much as the sea itself, in some ways. While the sea's inestimable power and changing moods awe and intrigue like no other force, the marshes stand down on human level, accessible, basic — primeval like nothing else. It is that oozy ancientness, including the smell of decay and new life and the essence of the sea itself, that brings me back time after time.

Part of my attraction stems from sheer exoticism; because I have only gardened inland, I am charmed by plant life on the marshes. Seeing expanses of marshland — between St. Simons and the mainland, for example — is as strikingly different from what I see back home in Atlanta as the oceans of wheat fields on the Kansas landscape.

Increasingly, for me, there is another pull to the coast. Just as there is something primeval about areas around oceans, there also is something primeval in the human need to be in these areas. All you have to do is look at the explosive growth at places like St. Simons, Hilton Head and Destin to understand the passion for life around the sea. In my case, the passion intensifies with age. Judging from the number of retirees I've met around here, I'm not alone.

My fifteen years along the banks of the Mississippi River, in East St. Louis, Illinois, were not nearly as affecting as my visits to the coast of Georgia. Of course, part of the difference is Big Muddy compared to the Atlantic. But I believe the increased time has as much effect as the increased water.

For the last eight years, whenever I've driven to the coast, I've pulled hunks of Spanish moss from trees, stuffed them into the car trunk and taken them back to my Atlanta garden. Much of what I've collected got snatched by nesting birds, but what is left thrives, tinges of green proving it is alive.

Also, I have worked hard to establish creeping fig on a brick wall in my garden, substituting that coastal favorite for Boston ivy. Each winter, the fig dies back but rises higher on the wall every spring — a reminder of the great walls of fig I've seen and loved in Charleston and Savannah.

A month or so ago, during a trip to Savannah, I pulled my car onto the shoulder near Thunderbolt and admired the marsh grasses. I picked up a couple of pieces and took them home. One grass had sawtooth edges that you can feel if you rub your fingers down the blade from the top. Another was rounded, with a hollow center. Unlike the Spanish moss, which lives in my garden even though Atlanta is way above the moss line in Macon, these grasses could survive only as souvenirs on a shelf in my writing room.

On this trip to the Golden Isles and McIntosh County, I am collecting no moss, no grasses. Reminders are no longer enough. This trip is the start of a hunt to buy a little piece of land by the marshes.

Like so many others, I now must have a place to go and enjoy as a counterpoint to my place in the city. Rural, quiet, primeval.

I want to know the language of the coast, learn about tidal creeks and mud fiddlers and salt pans. Cordgrass, needle rush and sea oxeye. Marsh aster. Some day soon.

August 16, 1997

UGA'S SACRED HEDGES

Athens, Georgia — Vince Dooley, studying the field intently as his Georgia Bulldogs lined up for another play that would lead to another touchdown last Saturday, managed a smile amid the heat of battle when I mentioned the Hedges.

As the crowd roar faded, we talked about how the hedges had been removed to expand Sanford Stadium's playing field and make way for Olympic soccer last year — and what would have happened if cuttings from the originals had not survived.

"I wouldn't be standing here today," Dooley replied instantly.

What? The University of Georgia's most revered football coach ever, now the school's athletic director and a talented gardener, to boot — run off over common privet hedge?

Well, I don't think so. But, Dooley's about the only official among those deciding to remove the hedges (they needed replacing, anyway) who could have survived Georgia fans' wrath; the fact is, there's something sacred about these plantings.

Fortunately for all concerned (including Atlanta Olympics chief and former Georgia defensive lineman Billy Payne), the hedges are looking real nice these days — a little more than a year after installation of the propagated plants, known as the "sons and daughters" of Hedges and as "Hedges II." The tradition they carry on dates back to 1929, when the originals were put in.

Anyone who's ever taken a chance on a special, valued plant in a garden — moving one to a different spot, pruning one severely, trying to grow a bright-light plant in low light — knows how good it feels when things work out fine.

Ray McEwen certainly does. The man who manages the stadium has a smile in his voice these days, saying the one thousand sons and daughters "have blended just like a good haircut" to create the green rectangle that, last Saturday, enclosed a Georgia winning field. "I think the project was a success. We've had no one who didn't like the new hedges."

McEwen says other schools (Auburn, for example) have planted their own, knowing how UGA's football power and glory grew between the hedges: "However, they haven't caught on. They don't offer the same mystique."

Mystique is mercurial. You might think that even the lowly privet hedge would sell like azaleas if people knew it was propagated from the original UGA hedges. It didn't work that way. More plants were propagated than UGA needed — a whole lot of backups. When it became clear the new plantings were doing OK, and the extras unneeded, they were put on sale. "We discovered that not many people were interested in privet," says McEwen. "We wound up throwing most of them away," as tending them was too costly.

Perhaps gardeners declined in droves to buy the propagated hedges because they realized that some things only work in certain places. The Hedges belong at UGA, as fans made clear when the beloved plants were removed for the Games. Just as many of us wouldn't dare try to make sushi at home, most lovers of the hedges are not interested in growing them in their own back yards.

Of course, we're talking about privet, which some gardeners consider a weed. Would more people have bought those extra plants if the hedges had been English boxwood — or cassine holly? Abelia? Juniper or elaeagnus?

We'll never know, of course. The hedges are what they are, and nobody's about to try to change them. Or remove them again any time soon.

September 27, 1997

BETTER THAN MY DOWNTOWN

Charleston — The warm, sunny weather was perfect for garden tours. Or, I should say, for garden tourists; Charlestonians were more likely to dig in their own dirt than attend the Charleston Garden Festival, a four-day event featuring tours, exhibits and lectures. "We hate it when the weather's this beautiful," one of the organizers confided with a laugh last weekend.

Enough of us out-of-towners sampled the festival to keep it humming. However, as always, the big show here was not the official tour of homes and gardens (as spectacular as some are), but the collective unofficial spaces throughout the city, especially those in the downtown historic district.

On and around Meeting Street near the Battery, for example, clumps of tourists got their kicks from "discovering" unofficial gardens tucked alongside unofficial homes. "Oh, come here, Betty!" I heard one woman shout to a friend. "Look at this; you're going to love this one." Betty did.

Looking through the wrought iron gate down the narrow space, I saw nothing exceptional about this one — a nice assortment of shade-tolerant plants, including ferns, azalea, rhododendron, camellia and a Charleston favorite, the cast iron plant. I decided neither the plants nor the garden's design created such delighted responses.

No, the magic here seems connected to other sources, including the pleasure of happening upon spaces that feel mysterious, secret, cozy. Sometimes these spaces are tiny, tucked away and barely visible from the sidewalk. Often they are framed by the city's many gates, arches, sides of neighboring homes. Sometimes they lie at the end of passageways that, with their own plantings or design, lead the eye.

There is something about a frame; that brick, metal or wood structure so enhances a space, making it a living photograph, much like those in New Orleans and Savannah.

Sitting in the Meeting Street Inn courtyard, I saw the frame work. Walkers stop by the inn's entrance — or, like characters in a movie, pass through the frame only to reappear a second later, pedaling and leaning backward. They then stare at the potted plants, the creeping-fig covered wall, the shrubs and small trees growing around the inn, which dates to 1874.

As much as anything, it is the ambience we respond to as we walk through the city's downtown neighborhoods. Old, lovingly tended homes and shops, streets friendly to pedestrians. Streets that feel good and safe.

First-timers from Atlanta, bracing for beggings when they walk the sidewalks here, always are pleasantly surprised at the absence of panhandlers, shouters and assorted other madding street distractors.

Visitors no doubt feel saftey in numbers; day and night, people fill downtown Charleston. And I don't think special attractions draw them; the city's main museum isn't much to see, for example — not nearly as interesting or informative as Atlanta's Cyclorama, depicting a Civil War battle.

Atlanta could build a big, fancy aquarium, redo Underground — again — and people still wouldn't be pulled downtown as they are pulled here.

Why? Partly because downtown visitors seek the same ambience that downtown residents do.

On her lovely piazza, lushed with green plants and elegant rugs, Katherine Daughtridge and I sipped cold drinks and talked about political will — and the absence of it. Laws against panhandling and playing loud "music" get enforced here. Unlike in downtown Atlanta, I never hear or feel one assaulting sound from a car with the windows down.

If those laws were not enforced, Daughtridge and I would have been forced inside to hear ourselves talk. And as in my hometown, downtown would be a place to shun.

October 11, 1997

GREEN SUMMERS OF HOME

Gloucester, Massachusetts — On one side of Atlantic Road, there is the ocean, sometimes crashing, sometimes gently splashing against seaweed-blackened rocks that slope upward to a row of rambling beach roses. On the other side of the road, houses and gardens facing the sea hunker down in New England's wintry late fall. The short summer's big shot of color is long gone, autumn's storied leaf shows a crisp memory.

Among the Atlantic Road residents are Peggy O'Neill and her husband, Pete Richards. I first visited their lovely garden last year, somewhat earlier in the season, when it was leafy and lush and blooming large. Now, the garden is fully in cold-weather mode, as are Peggy and Pete, who think of visiting warmer climes.

Coming here is like riding a horticultural time machine. While my roses back in Atlanta still are blooming and budding, as warm temperatures coax flowers from azaleas, Peggy's gardening (Pete's the appreciator) has come to a final chore: "Mainly, I'm putting it all to bed."

Yes, cold zaps Georgia sometimes, but there's nothing like a couple of pre-Thanksgiving days on Cape Ann, where gardens have gone into hibernation, to make you appreciate short, relatively mild Southern winters.

But mixed in with the appreciation is a little envy: Part of winter's charm is its bare beauty, its expansion of the garden. Winter gives us opportunity to see what cannot be seen during lush springs and summers. In cold climates like New England's, that opportunity grows, as down time is so much longer. The starker contrast between lushness and languor means the growing season here is more sharply defined than our Southern season — and in some ways more treasured, like anything so rare.

My gardening friends throughout New England have talked about their long winter's wait and the planting orgy that starts as soon as the ground thaws. Some cite the short growing season to explain their affinity for quick-hit, big-bang flower gardens rather than slow-growing, structured spaces featuring trees and shrubs. Others rely mainly on evergreens — hollies, junipers, pines — to provide permanently verdant landscapes, punctuated with a few pansies or geraniums for color.

For her part, Peggy O'Neill grows a range of plants and has built a garden that uses winter to great advantage. Here, where stones crop up everywhere (it's not for nothing that one of Cape Ann's towns is named Rockport), Peggy has had other stones hauled in to create a meditation garden, as inviting in winter as in summer. Among some of her rocks she has planted thyme and sedum; others provide stony backdrops for ornamental grasses that wave when the cold north winds begin to blow. Here and there, lamb's-ear still hangs on, and juniper creeping among the stones has gone gray and rust-colored. A marvelous, leafless weeping cherry stands like a monument among the rocks in the back garden. So many stones lend an air of timelessness in this cold gray season.

As for time to garden, Peggy acknowledges that Cape Ann's winters mean, "as soon as you plant, you want everything to be big immediately." But she also believes her lush season is long enough. Noting that her garden, which in summer includes geraniums, roses, tomatoes, sunflowers, poppies, usually gets full and green in May and stays that way until October, she says, "Four or five months is a long time. By then, I'm exhausted."

Back in the South, gardening the longer lush season could be even more exhausting. But we've learned to pace ourselves.

And live with our choices: As much as I love Cape Ann's long gray winter on the sea, Georgia's long green summer is home.

December 6, 1997

WILD PARADISE

Ossabaw Island, Georgia — It is a mere thirty-minute boat ride from Savannah, but this place takes you back eons. Back to where the wild things are. Alligators, pigs, deer, horses, Sicilian donkeys and more. Add to these the un-wild geese, peacocks and others, and you understand why Eleanor "Sandy" Torrey West sees parts of her garden nibbled away from time to time.

"A year ago, I went to Savannah and bought a whole bunch of wonderful plants," West tells me during a Saturday chat. "They (the animals) ate them all." But because she loves animals, as well as plants, West tells the story with a chuckle, concluding: "I didn't mind."

So goes the gardening life on Ossabaw Island, the 26,000-acre refuge twenty miles south of Savannah. West and other family members sold the barrier island to the state in 1978, and she has continued to live in the imposing Spanish Revival mansion her parents built in the 1920s.

With so much space to roam (the island is larger than Bermuda), the animal population flourishes. And forages. The donkeys and horses pull plants out by the roots, say experts who add there's just about nothing safe from the pigs. West recalls how, when garden club members admire her high-pruned camellias, she has to give browsing deer the credit.

There's nothing like a visit to this place to make you appreciate how easy some of us backyard gardeners have it, dealing with nothing more destructive than squirrels and chipmunks and cats. At the same time, there's nothing like a visit to make you appreciate the beauty of a place still unspoiled.

Touring with the Ossabaw Island Foundation (a nonprofit group that works to preserve the island) as the "spouse of" board member Lyn, I get my introduction to Ossabaw.

On a bumpy truck ride that reminds me of isolated country roads of long ago, several of us, including foundation board member Suzanne Williams and Lonice Barrett, commissioner of Georgia's Department of Natural Resources, marvel at the forest of palmettos, punctuated by pines, oaks, all dripping Spanish moss primevally. Here and there, a pig scampers.

Sightings abound. "Look! Look at that pine!" shouts Courtney Gaines, another board member, as we all snap to attention in the majestic face of an ancient specimen towering toward the slate-gray skies turning blue.

All along the way, we see much yaupon. Bamboo, wax myrtle. Way off the road, there; is that native azalea? So much to see, so much to wonder about in this sprawling island garden. And so much to learn. Barrett says one of his department's high priorities is an inventory of Ossabaw Island flora, a survey that probably will begin this summer.

Back at the mansion, there is another garden, far more formal; it is walled (the better to ensure that the plants don't become dinner). With a tiled courtyard. On this chilly January day, two great saucer magnolias threaten to burst into flower, while a pink rose apparently never stops. Creeping fig greens the pink wall, while red and white geraniums hang potted from a spiral iron staircase. This is the counterpoint to the wild island garden.

Such a rare place, this Ossabaw. "It's a paradise," says Carolyn Boyd Hatcher, president and CEO of the Georgia Conservancy.

"The plants and animals live in harmony except where man has messed it up."

A foundation board member, she, too, tours Ossabaw this day. And, as I do, Hatcher dreams of what she would do if she lived in this paradise: "I would have a vegetable garden, and of course I'd have a flower garden." Here she pauses, "But I would also just let the natural plants flourish."

The pigs'd like that.

January 31, 1998

. . . RESPONSE TO THE MOUNTAINS

Place of the Plant — For years, Lyn and I had felt the pull of the ocean, the salt marshes, dreamed of the wonderful life and gardening opportunities awaiting us on the coast. And for months, we traveled Georgia's eastern edge, from Savannah to McIntosh County to the Golden Isles, looking for our place.

We saw many, made no deals for any.

A couple of months ago, we decided a second home was not meant to be. At least, not now.

Last week, we bought a cabin in the North Georgia mountains. Way north, in McCaysville, a walk from Tennessee. Deep in the heart of Cherokee country.

What a surprise; we'll have an Appalachian spring. What a powerful demonstration of how life's plan changes right before your eyes, how you take roads today that were far, far away from yesterday's course.

True, our visits to the mountains always inspired. The woods, the native plants, the crisp air and sparkling streams repeatedly brought peace with a tingly edge. But, we figured a coastal get-away would come long before any move toward a mountain retreat.

That was before we saw the house that Mickey Galloway built, the stone-rich land it sits on, the mountains and water it views. One look (actually, two, as Lyn and I visited separately), and we were sold.

My drive north from Atlanta, through Cherokee County, past Ellijay, set the stage. On the day I went to look at the cabin, mist floated low over the mountains — a scene begging to be sketched in shades of gray, white, black and blue. At one point, the sun broke through, lighting up the mountainsides, making the still-sleeping trees glow like copper fennel.

The closer to the mountains I got, the more distinct each tree became, until, finally, when I reached the cabin, I felt in the mountains, a part of them. It felt good.

Just as a new relationship draws two people down a million conversational paths as they explore one another, this pine cabin in the woods pulls us in myriad directions as we anticipate our new love affair.

And what an affair it promises to be. Including a whole new gardening life.

I have heard that the area around here was known to the Cherokees as Place of the Plant. I will cultivate all I can to keep the name alive.

It helps that the area is a flora smorgasbord. The cabin looks over Fightingtown Creek, whose cool, fast waters flow past groups of ten-foot-tall rhododendron standing sentry along the stream's edge.

Mickey, his wife, Dionne, and neighbor Greg Crawford describe woods filled with native azalea, ferns, laurel, all manner of wildflowers and trees, including lots of hemlocks — a few of which Mickey already has donated to my new growing effort.

As spring turns to summer, I will see what I've heard about. As will Lyn, who, for the first time, is volunteering to actually get sweaty in the garden, helping build a rocky path to the creek. We shall see.

This new venture complements my Atlanta gardening. The two places will show differences, of course, but similarities, too. I am curious to see them all. My mountain garden will have more wild plants, I know, but the two spaces will share my love of serendipity.

Ironically, over the last several years, I have been connecting the two places, relieving friends of plants from these parts, putting them in my Atlanta garden: rattlesnake orchid, Japanese paper plant (naturalized in North Georgia), Jack-in-the-pulpit, trillium, bloodroot and others. Now, I will find out what it's like to live in a space where such plants just show up.

Just as I am discovering the excitement of becoming mountain man before coastal man.

March 21, 1998

fathers seeds ~ peas, corn, peanuts, grapes

Peas - pisum sativum

PART ELEVEN

RHYTHMS

Nothing affirms life more
than the element of change

~

VEGETABLES AGAIN

IN THIS NEW YEAR'S first blushes, promise springs eternal.

This is the year I keep a vow to my father and myself; I'll be growing food again.

Not enough to get me on any lists of biggest crops or biggest specimens, but at least enough to provide us a few good eats and save us from store-bought tomatoes.

It has been well over a decade since I grew anything to eat, other than herbs, and my father has never understood why I would use valuable ground to grow shrubs, trees and perennials.

In his garden in Meridian, Mississippi, he has grown some serious food, including corn, beans, greens, peas, okra, squash, tomatoes, grapes and peanuts. Eating from his garden is always a soulful treat.

At the end of one of our visits last year, my father dug out a little can from his toolshed and carefully picked from among his dried seeds some for me, making a starter kit: okra and watermelon seeds, peanuts, kernels of corn.

"You can get a good crop out of these," he said, as he handed me the container.

Recently, I've been looking at the can. It's white cardboard, with a red plastic top, labeled Food Club sun-dried California raisins, and it is stamped, "Sell by February 25, 1993."

Well, I'm not sure when I'll plant the seeds, and I'll not be growing peanuts, corn or watermelons among the nandina, pieris and bamboo. But the okra seeds will go into the ground. And I'll buy a few more seeds or seedlings to grow eggplant, peppers and tomatoes. Maybe as the season goes along, some others will inspire me.

Many readers have been inspiring and encouraging since I wrote about my father's garden last June, including Seiho Tajiri, Gerald Wade and John Yarbrough. They good-naturedly cajoled me to honor my father's wish — grow food.

"Steal a little space from your ornamentals and plant a little Ples Mae (my father's name) patch in your back yard," Yarbrough wrote in a note from Gainesville, Georgia.

OK, this is the year. Tips and advice are welcome.

When we talked on the telephone the other day, my father did not seem surprised to learn of my promised garden, and I did not bother to tell him that part of the way I convinced myself to grow food was to contemplate the beauty of some vegetable plants.

The eggplant, for example, grows a wonderful rich purple, and peppers, in addition to satisfying my addiction to spices, give a space great reds, yellows and greens. The foliage on both is attractive, too, as are okra's blossoms.

Perhaps I need not tell my father any of this. All along I've assumed he was growing food just for his stomach. Maybe it was for his eyes, too.

In any case, when we talked the other day, it was mostly about the advantages of growing our own: big flavor and little pesticide. "When you go to the market and pick up something, you don't know what you're getting," he said. "Even the store people don't know what's in it."

I'm not sure if he ever ate a store-bought tomato, and if this year's effort works out, I never intend to again.

There is some symmetry to my growing food again. The last time I did was when I lived in Atlanta in the 1970s, planting an ambitious garden that was much like my father's, including corn, beans, squash, tomatoes. . . .

I recall harvesting maybe three ears of corn, and the other crops bore pitifully little, as the spot I chose was not nearly sunny enough.

Fortunately, there's more sun in my garden these days, as there is in my life.

As for my eighty-four-year-old father, he sounded sunny and strong the other day, probably stronger than he is. He gardened almost none last year, blaming failing health and vagaries of weather.

But, perhaps buoyed by the spirit of resolve that flows so heavily this time of year, he looked ahead to planting and, characteristically, lauded the hard work and reward connected to it.

"Nothin's gonna come and get in your lap," he said. "You got to work for it."

And he shared a bit of wisdom that I must remember as I rejoin the ranks of vegetable people: "It's a risky run any way you go. Always be prepared to go back over it again if you mess up; if you fail, just plant again."

January 7, 1994

GARDEN DONE? NEVER

After working five years to get the garden established, stability still eludes the place. I know a garden is never finished, but I'm beginning to wonder if mine will even get a rest.

This is the year that my garden reaches its fifth birthday, my measure of the time it takes for plants to get comfortable with one another and with their spaces. So, watching the five-year mark approach in July, I felt a sense of ease. This is when I could start gardening in the slow lane, fine-tuning instead of furiously planting.

The fifth year is especially significant, because this garden is my first to reach that age, as I have spent decades moving from city to city as an itinerant journalist or house to house in search of a better place to live.

Thus, just as my gardens were coming of age, I was going someplace else, starting over.

But Peeples Street would be different; my garden here would be settled, approaching middle age, ready to retire on low maintenance. Maybe a nip with the pruning shears here, a tuck of ground cover around a stone there. A few separations of ferns and hostas. Easy Street.

Wrong. Year Five might as well be Year One. Older plants get moved and new ones put in for a variety of reasons, including bad light, the serendipity of my garden design, incredibly generous friends and simple greed and lust for something I don't have.

True, some of the plants that I put in five years ago have never moved, including several Japanese maples, a couple of pines, laurel, camellia, a corkscrew willow. (I didn't move any bamboo either, but then, it never needs help living all over the garden.)

Despite the stability of these and other plants, the world around them is shifting with great rapidity. Even as I celebrate the coming of the fifth year.

Across the front of the house, a row of azaleas had lived for at least fifteen years. Long enough, I decided. So in December I replaced them with hydrangeas, relishing their puffy blooms, which, like some women I know, grow more beautiful with age.

Penny McHenry, "the hydrangea lady," provided me some of her prized stock, and in early May I got my first blooms, blue as well as pink. Penny and I are conducting an experiment to determine whether my plants, in a different location, will bloom into November, as hers do.

An autumn fern in a hanging box on the porch just wasn't working out, dying back ugly in winter and taking forever to return. Lyn and I (she's voicing her plant choices more and more these days) decided that variegated ivy would work much better in that spot.

Celestine Sibley helped, bringing from her garden a sackful of the very ivy we wanted. Pieces of it now grow happily in several places indoors and out.

Apparently, the change in the hanging box was extraordinarily appealing. I climbed a stepladder one day to water the ivy, only to come face to face with a pair of doves that had taken up residence. Now, do I water the ivy and disturb a happy home, or not water it and risk losing the Celestine ivy? Yes, it was an easy decision. And fortunately, despite suffering a month without water, the ivy survived — a discovery I made in late April when the doves moved on to richer digs.

The changes continue. Now the hanging box's autumn fern and several others are planted behind the new hydrangeas, so that when the shrubs lose their leaves, the ferns can show through — that is if they choose to be truly evergreen, as their press kits claim.

I scattered vegetables among the ornamentals, making neighbors of collards and bamboo, of tomatoes, okra and banana shrub, eggplant and aucuba. Some of the veggies come from seeds I got from my father last year.

On a recent visit to Faye and Buddy Ward's lovely garden in Hartwell, Georgia, I came away with a trunkload of astilbe in various colors and heights. I found them a home around a volcano rock Harry Abel left on our porch last year as a Christmas gift. Nearby stands some new black bamboo from Sally and Bob Woo.

And, just the other day, Lyn and I stormed a nursery and bought three trees, having a clue where only one would go. That one, a paperbark maple, promising bright red and orange leaves in fall to complement its cinnamon-brown peeling bark, was destined for a Sahara-sunny spot near a back wall, replacing a kousa dogwood that had shrunk and sputtered. The kousa either had not read that it's supposed to appreciate sun, or it just drew the line at living on a desert. Anyway, it wound up in the shadier front garden.

Amazingly, the other two trees, a ginkgo and a green threadleaf Japanese maple, found homes where there seemed to be none. Isn't that always the case? We called the threadleaf Lyn's Mother's Day gift. Both newcomers are in the desert. So far, so good.

Given my continued planting and replanting, it was ironic to have Lyn report that a man recently asked her, "Does your husband really do a lot of gardening?"

Her reply: "Does the word 'addiction' mean anything to you?"

A brutal analysis of what I prefer calling the Five-Year Itch. It'll continue as long as we have gardening friends and a few dollars to spend.

May 27, 1994

FERTILE SOUTHERN EXCESS

Atlanta loves gardeners, but it sometimes has a strange way of showing it. Its balmy autumn and winter weather often beats California's (we have warmth and change of seasons). Dogwoods bloom in November. Azaleas flower in December and January. New growth appears long before spring.

Then, like a Venus fly trap enticing, then zapping, its prey, Atlanta turns brutally, suddenly cold — leaving gardens a mess, at least temporarily.

Warm. Rain. Cold. Freeze. Thaw. Warm. The cycle repeats. Rain, instead of being hailed as life-giving, instills fear as the forerunner of killer ice.

Now believing, hoping, the cycle is winding down, I increasingly take damage surveys. Call it a combination of cabin fever and prespring fever. I step over the wounded and the dead, the valiant plants that even in January were lush and flush but now lie frozen to mush.

Some of the victims die back each year, of course, as is their perennial habit. But their demise affects because they survive in good shape so long past their supposed prime, making me believe they'll live forever, or at least through the mild winter. But again this year, as in seasons past, winter pounced on them, catching them unawares.

In the front garden, near the fence, there is, or was, an acanthus every bit as beautiful as those I remember seeing down around Claxton, Georgia, a few years ago. After furiously putting out leaves through fall and early winter, the cool-loving perennial, whose large, lobed leaves inspired doodads on Greek columns, was felled when winter struck hard just after all the big-name groundhogs failed to see their shadows. Noble acanthus leaves and stems sprawled soggily, turning the color of ripe chinaberries.

Even the aptly named cast-iron plant gets raggedy in Atlanta's seesaw weather. Its leaves apparently freeze to brittle, then suffer tears and brownout. Still, they wave gamely in the breeze, waiting for reinforcements from underground. Soon.

And pansies, among the garden's toughest blooming plants, suffered recently. Their smiles faded to frowns as a blast of cold knocked their little faces to the ground. They'll be back.

Despite the casualties, I do not wish for a long, constant cold season. True, that would bring a degree of certainty: You reach a date, and your plants go down for the count until spring. No yo-yo.

But Southern weather is like Southern people. The meteorological volatility here seems to fit the region's historical emotional rawness, its fertile excess that showed up in my family and friends as too much talking, too much smoking, drinking, eating too many fat-laden foods.

The weather, like Southerners, stands out. It gets your attention, just as do rich Southern accents and architecture. For my part, the weather's destructiveness — in the garden, at least — is offset by its refreshing unpredictability, its absence of sameness.

Yes, it is true that places like Los Angeles and New York have varied weather, too. But in either it's difficult to find somebody who can fix good grits, chitlins or cracklin bread.

March 3, 1995

A MIND OF ITS OWN

There are times a garden does what it does, no matter what the gardener does. I'm in the middle of one of those times.

A couple of years ago, I cleared two little raised rectangles of the junipers that had been growing there for years and set out to turn the spaces into moss gardens.

I thought I was doing everything "right," including ensuring the spaces were not drenched in sun and keeping the moss plugs watered.

And, over the several months that I was building the gardens, I got a lot of help from friends who were trying to get rid of their mosses. Some would invite me to their yards, where I scooped up sheets of moss. Others would deposit their gifts in my yard if they happened to be in the neighborhood. I always kept a trowel in the car trunk, using it if I happened to find a nice stand of moss during walks in the woods.

After a while, I had woven a mighty fine quilt of moss, a patchwork whose pieces all had their stories, much like my garden of shrubs and trees, collected during my years of frequent travel. Here's a piece of moss I call Connie. Next to it is a huge chunk named Tom. Moss memories.

Two years later, I have even less moss in those spaces than I had when I started.

Birds and squirrels certainly have taken their toll on the soothing green moss bed, scratching and tossing it away by the chunk. And some of the moss died away. Still, I'd pursue my dream of two spare little verdant spaces if these were the only problems. But there is a nagging something else about those plots that tells me they simply are not meant to be moss gardens.

Maybe I was wrong in my sunlight assessment, failing to factor in the increased intensity during winter months when the trees are bare. Maybe the soil is too rich. Maybe I didn't keep it wet enough. Maybe the spaces are just wrong, for reasons I can never know. Maybe, maybe.

After a while we all get tired of maybes. Certainty is what we want, even as we realize life offers no guarantees. You get to that point, whether with lovers or with mosses.

Seeking certainty, I turned to stone. The would-have-been moss garden is in transition, becoming a rock garden.

By rock garden, I don't mean a couple of rocks with plants growing over, around and through them; I mean the same thing that Godfrey Barnsley meant back in 1841 when he moved his family to Bartow County, where he built a mansion called Woodlands. Reincarnated as Barnsley Gardens at Woodlands, it has beome a popular attraction near Adairsville, lushly planted and architecturally revealing in its roofless, ruined state. In front of the manor house, near the mesmerizingly beautiful boxwood parterre, are two piles of rocks. Just rocks, assembled in a natural fashion, growing a few little plants. They are the rock gardens, or rockeries, the model for my smaller-scale rock garden.

I began transforming one of my unsuccessful moss gardens (I put bamboo in the other space) into a rock garden about two months ago, lugging small stray rocks to the rectangle from various nooks and crannies in the garden. These new rocks joined the three larger ones I had set among the mosses.

Size or color or texture doesn't matter (I suspect rockery historians would say they should all look alike). Brown, white, red, gray — all are welcome. I've put in smooth ones, rough ones — quartz, river rocks, granite, fieldstones. Volcanic rocks will come.

Now that friends have seen the plan, they are helping to build the garden, just as some had with the mosses. Contributions have begun. I now have several Wade rocks, brought back from a trip to the North Georgia mountains. Recently, I got a Jill rock from South Carolina. A smooth, round one I fished out of the Potomac River reminds me of my feverish years in the nation's capital.

One by one, the rocks cover a patch of moss. I am in no hurry. Part of me is giving the moss time to yell, "Stop. I'll grow." Another part of me savors changing an unnatural situation to a natural one: The moss obviously was out of its element; the rocks are fitting in without complaint (and without special needs, I might add).

This experience is, in some ways, a microcosm of the construction of any garden. Or the deconstruction-reconstruction of any space.

I will think of all this as a kind of return to naturalness. It is as if I fought nature in an effort to harness it and display it in my yard, on my terms. On a far grander scale, Californians carve out spaces on hillsides to build showy homes. And Carolinians build rich dwellings from which they can toss stones to the ocean. In the end, we all fight battles we can only lose.

For now, I have ended the struggle, at least the moss struggle. And I have been reminded, again, that part of the ongoing relationship between gardener and garden is learning to live in dynamic harmony — moving, adding, shaping and taking away. But always with mutual respect.

May 19, 1995

NO SEEDS OF CERTAINTY

With October running out of days, I guess it's time for me to give up; the ginger lily apparently doesn't feel like blooming this year.

I've waited and waited, checking for buds every day or so, incredulous that, for the first time since I planted it about six years ago, the plant will put out no creamy-white blooms, offer no fragrant greeting from half a block away. What a strange autumn. Complete with a Georgia hurricane.

The season seemed ordinary enough at first. The hardy begonia, which had been growing all summer but not flowering — and who blames it? — felt a few cool days and was inspired to thrust up many pink blooms.

But the ginger lily did nothing but grow foliage. I watched as it got tall and fell over, budless.

On the other side of the garden, a foxglove, bare through spring and summer, started to bloom in October, purplish and white, proving yet again that plants often pay no attention to books or calendars that purport to gauge their bloom times.

Knowing that no plant necessarily blooms by the clock, I was not concerned in early August when not even a bud had appeared on the ginger lily. But I began to worry a bit when friends began showing off their blooms.

Beth Gross telephoned one day in late August to report that her lily was in full flower. Curious, I went by to see it. Indeed, the plant, growing energetically in an open space in her southwest Atlanta garden, was cutting up, filled with a dozen blooms whose sweet smell recalled my own lily days the way seeing somebody's British sports car makes me think of youthful summers when I too had one.

"Isn't that a wonderful fragrance?" Beth asked innocently, realizing not at all how much she was making me long for just one little white bloom on my own plant.

"Yes" was all I said.

Then, in September, when I stopped in to see Bob and Sally Woo at Oriental Art on Roswell Road, I noticed that Sally had cut the bud cluster and about six inches of stem off one of her lilies and placed it in water in a little vase on the shop counter. A great, fragrant idea. Wasting none of that fragrance, Sally places spent blooms in a bowl, creating a potpourri that remains potent for months.

"See? This still smells good," said Sally, showing me the browned blooms.

"Yes," I said.

Looking at portions of a plant close-up and often, you see what you've never seen before. Sally pointed out that several of the little buds in the cluster produced one flower as usual, then went on to produce another. We both had thought that once a flower bloomed and died, no more came from that bud.

Learning from this flower only emphasized the absence of blooms on my own plant. Ironically, my garden has a barren lily in the same year that it had wisteria blooms for the first time — on a six-year-old plant.

Those two events are one example of the balance that takes place in a garden. Further, the ginger's not blooming corresponds to the growing density of the tree it grows under, a saucer magnolia. Several years ago I pruned the tree to admit light and air. Since then, it has become so thick, rain barely reaches the ground under it.

Alas, as the tree flourishes, the ginger lily fails to flower.

I take this as a sign to prune the magnolia just after it flowers in the winter. That, I hope, will let the lily bloom again next year. At the same time, I know the tree may wait until spring to bloom. And that it may not be the problem anyway.

This year without the sweet smell of ginger lily sends a message for life: Certainty does not grow in gardens.

October 20, 1995

LETTING THE GARDEN GO

Those of us who've grown both plants and children often see similarities between the two. For one thing, we're afraid to leave either home alone. Also, each is different; I could no more choose a favorite plant than I could a favorite daughter among the five Lyn and I have.

Plants, like children, vary, one from another. Therefore, no matter what the manuals say, you have to adjust your parenting to the individuals' needs, desires, coping abilities, temperaments, moods, ages — and more factors than you can sometimes count. While your eight-year-old may say she doesn't want to go to school because her best friend took up with another girl, and that life is ruined, her younger sister, in the same situation at the same age simply makes friends with someone else, without skipping a beat — or even mentioning the falling-out.

The difference is no more explainable than the reason one plant lives for years in one spot while right next to it another one of the same type just dies away.

With the children and the plants, you always ask if you're doing enough, how much you should do, how much you can do to make life better.

As a parent and a gardener, I've always seen those questions summing up the unavoidable tension between our wanting to give enough and needing not to give too much. Between paying too much attention and not paying enough.

This tension becomes no easier to relieve, no matter how at ease many parents today seem, compared to their grandparents. Sharing the sweet burden of parenting links generations.

The other night, one of our daughters telephoned to talk through her latest dilemma. Her seven-year-old daughter had been invited to visit a pal after school. No problem, until our daughter learned the babysitter was just thirteen and was responsible also for a third youngster.

What to do? Say no and disappoint her daughter and make the other girl's parents wonder why their place wasn't good enough to visit? Say yes and worry for several hours whether something awful would happen?

Maybe men worry less about such matters, or maybe our son-in-law simply worries less than our daughter. In any case, he had no problems with the visit. Lyn and I listened as our daughter figured out her course. She let her daughter go.

After listening to her wrestle herself toward this decision, I thought of how analogous her letting go was to my letting my garden fend for itself for several weeks in September and October.

If ever there is a time to do nothing in a garden, this is it. No raking (leaves just keep falling), no pruning (growth has mostly stopped anyway). But no watering? Yes. So, although we had two, three — I lost count — weeks without rain, I refused to unfurl the hose. I let go.

No, I didn't stop gardening; I let the garden be independent, just as our daughter let her daughter be.

I took my daily walk through the garden, trying to ignore the record harvest of acorns littering the walks, the dried up purple coneflowers, blue balloon flowers, four o'clocks, phlox. Too, I resisted raspy threats to die whispered by ferns as I passed. Survive, I said.

Everything did, making me wonder if I'd been doing too much. Similarly, our granddaughter's visit turned out okay, our daughter grudgingly acknowledged, making no promise to let her go again.

Last Sunday, I stopped letting the garden go. I spent about six hours, sweeping the walk, pruning away the dried perennials, pulling weeds. Watering.

Perhaps, I could have let go for a lot longer time; the plants probably would have survived, and the acorns and pecans eventually would have been walked away or eaten by squirrels.

I stopped letting go not because the garden needed me. I needed it.

October 19, 1996

AWASH IN PEACE

Water, in any form — flowing, dripping, cascading, bubbling, still — adds character and personality to a garden like nothing else can. Considered one of the essential elements of Japanese gardens, along with plants and stone, water works well in any space on earth.

Throughout the year, water weaves its magic in my garden, soothing, exciting, creating — like bonsai — miniatures of larger scenes in nature. In autumn and winter the magic is more intense, as the leaves fade from trees and shrubs, along with the flowers, opening up the garden, allowing me to more clearly see and appreciate water's wonder.

Five or so years ago, I put in my first water feature, a little pond. And I do mean little, about four feet by two — one of those irregularly shaped preformed polyurethane ones sold at nurseries. My attachment for it goes way beyond the simple pleasure I get from just staring at fish rippling still water.

I feel a special fondness for this little piece of water because each time I look at it, I remember the day I dug its hole. A Sunday on which I was fighting the flu. In sad shape, I walked out and looked at the little pond, knowing I couldn't dig out the hard, red clay in the condition my condition was in. I took my pick and shovel from the shed and poked a shallow hole or two — just to get a feel for the project. For later. Next thing I knew, I had dug a pond some two feet deep. I continued, putting a layer of sand on the bottom of the hole, leveling the molded pond as I filled it with water.

When it was all over, and the dollar-apiece goldfish were swimming happily, I discovered the flu was gone; it was a miracle, one repeated over and over for anyone who puts holes in the dirt — for water or plant. Gardening heals.

Having found deep joy in still water, I soon after discovered the aural beauty of water running through bamboo onto a stone basin: a tsukubai, designed and installed by Harry Abel. The sound of water on stone can wash away a whole lot of clutter gathered during a day. It is a primeval therapy.

And now, I spend more time with the water as the garden drifts toward winter and space becomes barer and barer. Water no longer competes with spring and summer bloomers and with lush foliaged deciduous neighbors.

The spicebush that stands right in front of the pond has turned its leaves yellow and dropped them, opening up a line of sight from the kitchen. Too, the cosmos is long gone, and the zinnias have wound down, no longer sending up waves of brilliant red blossoms that were breathtakingly beautiful but also took away the view of the pond. Gone are the black-eyed Susans and the lilies and the coneflowers, purple and white. All had surrounded the pond, doing a gorgeous job of attracting butterflies but concealing the water and the fish that look so happy eating algae, pond plants or an errant earthworm (I tried feeding them store-bought fish food once, but they apparently prefer their own home-grown victuals.

On the other side of the back garden, the tsukubai stands even more majestic than ever, its bamboo head and spout now weatherworn to a fine gray, its rock basin and those rocks surrounding it greenish with moss. Certainly, part of its attitude stems from its annual exposition, uncovered by the mock orange and the native azalea and the perennial flowers that insist on boogeying to loud blooms night and day.

Finally, I can hear the tsukubai saying, it is quiet time. Yes, whispers the pond. Our time.

November 16, 1996

CLEAN SWEEP

Having finally decided to clear my garden of fallen leaves instead of letting them lay and decay, I couldn't wait until spring; the cleanup had to come sooner. So, during a recent week, I gave myself to the task.

It was some of the hardest, dirtiest work I've done in a long time. Maybe since I dug out the dwarf bamboo. Or the ivy. Or the liriope. All those were difficult, but gathering what seemed like millions of leaves seemed tougher. The result, however, already has been strangely rewarding.

First, my family reacted as if, in clearing the garden of leaves, I had suddenly stopped eating spaghetti and tomato sauce with my fingers. Or going to the bank in my underwear.

Touring with me on Sunday, Lyn and our daughter Leslie heaped praise on the newly clean space. "I'm so glad you did this," said Leslie. "It's truly inspiring. And now I can see the plants."

Lyn said, "What a wonderful change you've made. Now the truth can be told: I had gotten to the point it wasn't fun walking in the garden with all those leaves piled up everywhere. You've made it fun again."

Well. You just never know what people are thinking. Even those closest to you. Here I was assuming they understood my natural gardening, leaving the leaves where they fell, forestlike. But no. All the while, they were hoping I'd clear the ground, so they could see what was growing in the garden.

After I got over the feeling that I was being welcomed back to civilization after a long absence, I had to concede the new look was better. The brown leaves could not compete with the dark loam as a background for the greens of the pines and the banana shrub and aucuba and all the other evergreens. Or for the coral-bark Japanese maples that seemed on fire above the newly visible black earth.

What a price I paid for this beauty. Admittedly, I did make it hard on myself; it had been too long since I did a total cleaning of the garden. Meantime, leaves from our tulip tree and saucer magnolia had fallen like raindrops, as had those from neighbors' pecan trees. But the greatest contributor by far is the giant tree next door, the pre–Civil War oak.

The most active tree I've ever seen, it petulantly spits down acorns by the barrel throughout the fall, gradually throwing off leaves at the same time and not going completely bare until after Christmas. This tree covers a whole lot of ground over a whole lot of time.

Of course, its thick growth and wide canopy make it a fantastic cooling machine in summer. Those who rake must do some backaching work in exchange for the benefits, however. A workfare oak, this is.

It and the rest of the trees had piled up enough leaves, seeds, fruit and other tree parts in my garden over the last several years to fill some fifty garbage bags. My compost piles now look like they're on steroids. Using a tiny rake, I navigated small spaces, snaring piles of leaves. I scooped with a dust pan, with my bare hands, marveling at what I uncovered. Fiddleheads coiled to unfurl into fern fronds. Mint that had never died back. Hydrangea canes pushing through the earth already, along with peony and hosta.

Yes, a cleaned-up garden is a beautiful sight. Lyn thinks even the fish are liking the new look, swimming closer to the pond surface. I know the robins have been enjoying feasts of newly exposed earthworms.

Unfortunately, squirrels, too, find the clean space appealing. They cavort with more than their usual frenetic energy, digging and gnawing, their tails gesturing obscenely. But even these tree-dwelling rodents cannot make me a leaf-leaver again. I'm committed to clean.

February 8, 1997

LEAVING PARADISE

Sara Ham of Fayette County, Georgia, is getting ready to leave the garden she's spent two decades building. She and her husband, Lin, who has a debilitating illness, both in their seventies, are moving to a smaller space, paring down their lives.

Any gardener can easily understand the difficulty in leaving a garden heavily invested with time, energy and love. For many of us, the pain is eased by the knowledge that we are going on to new spaces that are larger or more interesting. For Sara Ham that is not so.

"This place has so much and is so much fun," she said, noting that her new smaller space at a cluster home "will be a challenge." It is in this challenge that she must find solace, the challenge of converting the new space into something evocative of the verdant two acres she is leaving.

It's paradise. Carved out of the woods. Lin, a master craftsman, built the house, whose naturally beautiful West Coast cedar and Tennessee field stone complement the garden.

The other day, Sara, of small stature and lithesome grace, took fellow master gardener Mary Newcome and me on a walk through her garden — one of many walks she has taken lately as part of a long good-bye.

Against the house grows a climbing hydrangea, fourteen years old. A kousa dogwood, now in glorious bloom, grows just off the patio in a tall bed of azaleas. Down by the lake, between the sweet gum and the pine, in front of the daylilies, hostas flow around azaleas, an idyllic scene that made us all stop and feel. We moved on to what used to be a huge Japanese maple. Once ten feet tall, it now stands only about a foot high, whittled down by a beaver.

Yes, the critters Sara has known during her twenty years with this garden could fill a little zoo. Her recollection of separate encounters with two copperheads (she dispatched both snakes, one with a hoe, one with a rifle) amount to a metaphor for the difficulty of building a garden from scratch. It wasn't easy.

In laying the path that winds through the front grove, which includes spectacular ten-year-old rhododendron, ten-foot-tall azalea, buckeye, Canadian elm, anise, hydrangea, Sara and Lin poured and laid 134 stones that weigh 34 pounds apiece. Moving them around no doubt took its toll on Sara's knees, one of which was replaced last July. You'd never know that, however, as she ably led us down the path, where we stopped to admire the hemlocks.

"These were the first trees I bought," Sara said. "I bought ten, for a dollar apiece. Two lived." Now there are fourteen more, added about eight years ago.

Our walk takes us across a little stream, along whose banks grow Christmas ferns, curly ivy, mahonia and leucothoe. On the other side is the site of what normally would be Sara's bustling vegetable garden, planted in twelve raised beds. Not this year; she's leaving too soon.

This sunny area is not barren, however; asparagus, daisies, iris, larkspur and red hot poker thrive in side beds. After tasting a few asparagus spears — giving true meaning to the term, garden-fresh — we launch into a discussion of the bright-red sea of poppies.

Sara began growing the poppies ten years ago and was immediately intrigued by them. Easy to understand when you see their brilliant color, followed by the golfball-sized seed pods that look like green domes, each capped with a golden brown roof in sunburst pattern.

Stroking one of the poppies in full bloom, she said, "He bows his head until the day he's going to bloom, and then he turns his face to the heavens and says, "Glory!"

To be sure, seeing all those poppy faces was a glorious sight. As was the entire tour.

Sara will take many walks between now and next week, when she and Lin move. As difficult as the last stroll will be, she leaves with as much gratitude as sadness. Says Sara: "I appreciate my Heavenly Father's allowing me to have this for twenty years. It's been wonderful."

May 10, 1997

SUMMING UP

Just as a half-century in life is a good time to take stock of how you've lived, what you've achieved, this halfway point in the year seems appropriate for measuring how well — or poorly — the garden's grown.

The most hurting thing in my garden was losing the mimosa again to the electrical workers who have to cut it down each time they open the underground wiring box next to the tree (unable to read, the mimosa violates the warning on the metal box against growing closer than ten feet). The mimosa was just recovering from its last losing battle with the saw when the box had to be opened again this year, dooming the tree before it was able to bloom.

Now, as I drive around the region, admiring the mimosa's beautiful pink and white blossoms amid ferny leaves dancing in the breeze, I can only imagine the feathery touch and sweet fragrance of those powder-puff blossoms that, years ago, provided many of us southerners a taste of nectar and a bookful of lasting memories.

The gutsy mimosa is coming back for the third time, like an aging boxer refusing to stay down for the count: Two feet of new growth rise from the stump. Knowing the odds against it, I have taken steps against being mimosa-less again.

I collected one of the beleaguered tree's seedlings and put it in a bonsai tray, where it survived the winter and seems happy on the side porch. While I have grown bonsai for years as simply a way of re-creating a larger scene in nature, this is the first time I have grown one as a kind of preservation effort. The mimosa bonsai has put on fine new leaves, which, like its parent's, close in darkness and rain. I will know my effort succeeds when I see blooms.

No chance for success with the rosemary that I'd lusted after and finally got last year at the State Farmer's Market (after months of circling this hardy shrub that had survived winter untended, I finally was able to buy it when the owner returned to open her business in the spring of 1996). After a good start in my garden, the plant died slowly, branch by branch, finishing itself off last winter — the only rosemary in my garden to die this year. It probably would have lived had I left it where it was. Sad and scary how change can sometimes kill a thing.

On the food front, most of my potted crops resemble bedraggled troops, begging for a little R and R.

My tomato plant was beaten leafless by a hailstorm and still has not recovered. Same for the cayenne pepper. The okra, planted way too soon, it turns out, finally has decided to warily reach up. The poor peach tree bloomed beautifully and put out a tasteful number (read "five") of little peaches. One by one, they all dropped off, even before the squirrels could get them.

There is some good news. Though not defeated, the dwarf bamboo's on the run. Two pairs of worn-out pruning shears tell me to never get complacent with this stuff. This is my second season of battling it, having dug out as much as I could and cut the tops off the rest. Still, I patrol the garden, knowing that some unsuspecting shrub or perennial will be ambushed by the little plastic grass masquerading as friendly groundcover.

I keep a vigilant eye, also, on the brick wall, making sure the Boston ivy that once covered it stays gone. I dug it out last fall and have seen only an occasional shoot dashing up from some deep shred of a root.

To be sure, my midyear survey finds my garden looking vigorous and feeling good — overall. Yet, as in a midlife check, I know what goals haven't been met. And hope there's time to reach them.

July 7, 1997